SIXTH GRADE SURVIVAL GUIDE

Exam Prep, Fun Learning Hacks, and Practical Classroom
Strategies to Conquer Sixth Grade Like a CHAMPION!

Bobbie Anderson Jr

Thank you for buying our book and supporting our mission to provide accessible resources for everyone!

Instructions for Word Search Puzzles

- Hidden words are key vocabulary of each chapter
- Some words are combined. For example, "sixth grade" is hidden as "sixthgrade".
- Words are hidden in forward, horizontal, vertical, in reverse, and four diagonal directions (top-left, top-right, bottom-left, bottom-right).
- STUCK? The parenthesis shows combined words.

To avoid any potential bleed-through while solving word search puzzles with certain pens or markers, simply place a blank sheet of thicker paper behind the page you're working on.

This is more than just a book; it's a middle school confidence-building resource that supports you every step of the way. From exam prep, learning hacks, and practical classroom strategies for your success, it's the ultimate tool for conquering sixth grade like a CHAMPION!

Each chapter ends with a fun word search puzzle that reinforces key concepts, making learning enjoyable and helping you retain knowledge effectively.

you got this !

Table of Contents

BELONGS TO

Chapter 1

How to Handle the First Day of Sixth Grade Like a Pro

Welcome to sixth grade, superstar! This is a big year—you're officially in middle school (or maybe the last year of elementary), and everything feels a little bigger, newer, and maybe even a bit overwhelming. It's normal to feel nervous, excited, or a mix of both. But don't worry—you've got this! The first day of sixth grade is a chance to start fresh, meet new people, and show the world how amazing you are. This chapter is packed with tips, ideas, and real-life scenarios to help you crush your first day and set the tone for an awesome year. Let's get started!

1. Plan Ahead and Be Prepared

The night before, pack your bag with everything you need: notebooks, pencils, lunch, and any school forms. Check your schedule if you have one, and lay out your clothes so your morning is stress-free.

Real-Life Scenario:

Last year, you forgot to pack your math workbook on the first day and had to borrow paper from a friend. This time, you double-check your bag the night before. When your teacher says, "Take out your math book," you're ready to go, and it feels great.

2. Arrive Early and Explore

If you're in a new school, arriving early gives you a chance to find your classroom, figure out where the lockers are, and get familiar with your surroundings.

Real-Life Scenario:
You get to school 15 minutes early and find your homeroom teacher's door. Along the way, you spot the cafeteria and even say hi to a couple of kids from last year. Knowing where to go makes you feel more confident when the bell rings.

3. Bring a Positive Attitude
Walking into sixth grade with a smile and a positive mindset can make all the difference. Even if you're nervous, act confident—it will help you feel that way for real.

Real-Life Scenario:
You're a little anxious about meeting your new teacher. Instead of hiding in the back, you smile and say, "Good morning!" when you walk in. Your teacher smiles back, and you already feel more at ease.

4. Pay Attention to New Routines
Middle school (or upper elementary) often comes with new rules, schedules, and ways of doing things. Listen carefully when your teachers explain procedures like switching classes, using lockers, or turning in homework.

Real-Life Scenario:
Your science teacher explains the lab safety rules, and you write them down in your notebook. When the first experiment comes up, you're the one who remembers not to touch the equipment until the teacher says it's okay. Everyone's impressed by your responsibility!

5. Introduce Yourself and Make Connections
In sixth grade, you might have classmates you don't know yet. Take the opportunity to introduce yourself and start building friendships.

Real-Life Scenario:
You're sitting next to someone new in English class. You say, "Hi, I'm Alex. What's your favorite book?" They reply, "I love fantasy stories!" You bond over your love of Percy Jackson and decide to sit together at lunch.

6. Write Down Your Schedule
With new classes, different teachers, and maybe even switching rooms, it's easy to get confused. Keep a copy of your schedule in your notebook or phone so you always know where to go.

Real-Life Scenario:
You accidentally head to the gym instead of the library for your first elective. Luckily, you have your schedule handy and quickly find the right place. Crisis averted!

7. Be Open to New Things
Sixth grade often comes with new opportunities like clubs, sports, or electives. Say yes to trying something new—it could turn into your favorite part of the year.

Real-Life Scenario:
Your friend convinces you to try out for the debate team, even though you're nervous about speaking in front of people. You join, and by the end of the year, you've won a team award and feel more confident than ever.

8. Stay Organized
Between homework, projects, and activities, sixth grade can get busy fast. Use a planner or app to keep track of assignments, due dates, and after-school plans.

Real-Life Scenario:
Your math teacher assigns a worksheet due Thursday, and your social studies project is due Friday. You write both in your planner and set aside time to work on each. When Friday rolls around, you're the only one who isn't rushing to finish at the last minute.

9. Eat Lunch With Someone New
Lunch can feel a little awkward on the first day, especially if you're in a new school. Look for someone who seems friendly or is sitting alone and invite them to join you.

Real-Life Scenario:
You see a kid from your homeroom sitting by themselves. You walk over and say, "Mind if I sit here?" They smile and say, "Sure!" By the end of lunch, you've both discovered you're in the same math class.

10. Ask Questions
If you're confused about something—like where a classroom is or how to use a locker—don't be afraid to ask a teacher, classmate, or even an older student. Everyone was new once and knows how it feels.

Real-Life Scenario:
You can't figure out how to open your locker, and you're starting to panic. You ask the person next to you, and they show you how to turn the dial. Problem solved, and you've made a new friend in the process.

11. Be Kind to Yourself
The first day of sixth grade doesn't have to be perfect. If you make a mistake, don't sweat it—it's all part of learning and growing.

Real-Life Scenario:
You accidentally bring your gym shoes to math class, and everyone laughs. Instead of feeling embarrassed, you laugh too and say, "At least I'll be ready to run from tough problems!" Your humor turns the moment into a fun memory.

12. Reflect on the Day
At the end of the first day, take a few minutes to think about what went well and what you're excited for tomorrow. Thinking positively can boost your confidence for the year.

Real-Life Scenario:
You think about how you met two new friends, found all your classes, and even remembered to turn in your summer reading assignment. You feel proud and ready to tackle day two.

Final Thought
The first day of sixth grade might feel big and new, but it's also a fresh start full of exciting opportunities. By being prepared, staying positive, and embracing new experiences, you'll show yourself and everyone else that you're ready for this next adventure. So take a deep breath, smile, and step into sixth grade with confidence. You've got this!

```
M I N A X C D S J Y A B Y N Y W O A T A K X P
H T R O S D O N Q Q B L S E F R Y L A N X I L
L M H Q N C B H O W B G C Q G O K C Z I T V X
R I O I Y S H S L C V Z Y A T V T V I V I G N
O H K Q E W M E Q K Q X N X W C M L A K C J Z
U C R K C D W R D X E I M X E S R T C Q Q I Q
T H E I Q D B F Z U Z Y C L N P G Q A L R X M
I P N J X L B A V E L J F O M G C F B M B J D
N A L P K H N H D M Y E I H T B S T A R T I A
E U H E C V A F M N R T N J W V Z F K F B E S
S Z R Y K T Q M K B C P O S I T I V E W C A L
Z R W Q P R O U Q E C C X S S B N G C C C E U
N Q A D I K U L N Z E P K E H G C J U M A W N
D Q F N R Z I N U C O C V N W C J W L J Q F H
A G U R U Y O K I Z F I Q A L Z G X R B A T Y
T J S P A C Y B D K T A N L O R V P O L L V C
T B S X B Q A W E C O Z E V M S E A R L Y P T
I Y K C M W E D E S D G X F R L P O L V I C V
T P B H E O J L M W Q D I N N F I E B P A V A
U U O S U K E N J P B N P D L S G B H B Z K M
D W O Y T Q X U X F M Y H F D T V Q N N P X H
E M U V R E X E T R B Z S C X N K N K K L H W
E M I N Q M Z K G S I X T H G R A D E P P U W
```

attitude	fresh	reflect
awesome	kind	routines
connections	organized	schedule
early	plan	sixthgrade (sixth grade)
electives	positive	start

Chapter 2

How to Pick the Right Friends in Sixth Grade

Hey there, sixth grader! Choosing the right friends can be one of the most important parts of your year. Sixth grade is a time when friendships can change. You're meeting new people, trying new things, and figuring out who you are. The friends you choose can make your year awesome—or pretty stressful. But how do you know who the "right" friends are? In this chapter, we'll dive into tons of tips, ideas, and real-life sixth-grade scenarios to help you find and stick with the kind of friends who bring out the best in you. Let's get started!

1. Look for Friends Who Share Your Interests

The best friendships often start with shared interests. If you love basketball, drama club, or gaming, spend time with people who like those things too.

Real-Life Scenario:

You notice a kid in your homeroom wearing a jersey from your favorite basketball team. At lunch, you sit next to them and say, "Did you watch the game last night?" They grin and say, "Yeah, it was awesome!" By the end of lunch, you've found someone who gets your love for the sport.

2. Find Friends Who Support You

A true friend is someone who lifts you up, not tears you down. Look for people who cheer you on, celebrate your successes, and stand by you when things get tough.

Real-Life Scenario:

You're nervous about trying out for the school musical, but your friend says, "You've got a fantastic voice! You'll crush it!" Their support gives you the confidence to give it your best shot.

3. Notice How They Treat Others

How someone acts around others says a lot about them. A person who is kind and respectful to teachers, classmates, and even strangers is more likely to be a good friend.

Real-Life Scenario:

During gym class, you see a classmate help someone who tripped and fell. Later, you partner with them for a project and realize they're just as thoughtful to you. That's the kind of friend you want in your life.

4. Be Careful Around Drama

Middle school can bring more drama—rumors, arguments, and cliques. If someone loves stirring up trouble or pulling you into drama, they might not be the best friend for you.

Real-Life Scenario:

A group of kids you hang out with starts gossiping about another classmate. It makes you uncomfortable, so you decide to spend more time with your other friend who avoids that kind of talk. Suddenly, your days feel a lot less stressful.

5. Look for Friends Who Let You Be Yourself

The right friends accept you for who you are. If you feel like you have to act differently to fit in, they're probably not the right crowd.

Real-Life Scenario:

You love drawing comics, but one group teases you about it. Another friend says, "That's so cool! Can I see?" You realize that being with people who appreciate your interests feels way better.

6. Be Open to New Friendships

Occasionally, the individuals you once considered your closest companions may begin to distance themselves. That's okay—it's part of growing up. Be open to meeting new people who share your current interests and values.

Real-Life Scenario:

You and your old best friend don't have the same lunch period this year, so you start sitting with a new group. At first, it feels weird, but soon you discover that one of them shares your love of coding, and you bond over creating a game together.

7. Pay Attention to How You Feel Around Them

The right friends make you feel happy, confident, and safe. If you feel anxious, ignored, or uncomfortable around someone, it's worth thinking about whether they're a good match for you.

Real-Life Scenario:

You notice that after spending time with one group, you feel drained because they argue a lot. Meanwhile, another friend always makes you laugh and feel good about yourself. You start choosing to hang out with the friend who brings out your smile.

8. Find Friends Who Challenge You (In a Good Way)

The best friends don't just agree with everything you say—they challenge you to grow and think in new ways.

Real-Life Scenario:

You always avoid speaking in class because you're nervous. One day, your friend says, "You should share your idea—it's really good." You take a deep breath and raise your hand, and your teacher loves your answer. Your friend's push helps you grow.

9. Stand Up for What Matters

Sometimes, being a good friend means speaking up when someone isn't acting kindly. If your friend says or does something hurtful, don't be afraid to call them out (nicely).

Real-Life Scenario:
Your friend makes a joke about someone's clothes, and you say, "That's not cool. How would you feel if someone said that about you?" They apologize, and you both learn something about kindness.

10. Keep a Balanced Friendship

The best friendships are equal—both people give and take. If you're always helping someone with their problems but they're never there for you, it's not balanced.

Real-Life Scenario:
You always listen to your friend vent about their day, but when you try to talk about your worries, they brush you off. You realize you deserve a friend who listens as much as they talk, so you start spending more time with others who value your feelings.

11. Don't Be Afraid to Walk Away

If someone treats you badly, makes you feel small, or pressures you into doing things you don't want to do, it's okay to walk away. You deserve friends who respect and care about you.

Real-Life Scenario:
A friend dares you to cheat on a test, and when you refuse, they call you boring. You decide you don't need that kind of negativity and start hanging out with people who share your values.

12. Celebrate the Friends You Have

Once you find great friends, appreciate them! Say thank you, spend time together, and let them know how much they mean to you.

Real-Life Scenario:

Your friend helps you practice for your spelling bee, so you surprise them with a homemade thank-you card. They grin and say, "This is awesome!" Little gestures like this make your friendship even stronger.

Final Thought

Choosing the right friends in sixth grade is about finding people who make you feel happy, confident, and understood. By looking for kindness, honesty, and shared interests, you'll build friendships that make this year unforgettable. Remember, it's not about having a million friends—it's about finding the ones who truly care about you. So go out there, be yourself, and surround yourself with people who bring out the best in you. You've got this, sixth-grader!

Chapter 2 How to Pick the Right Friends in Sixth Grade

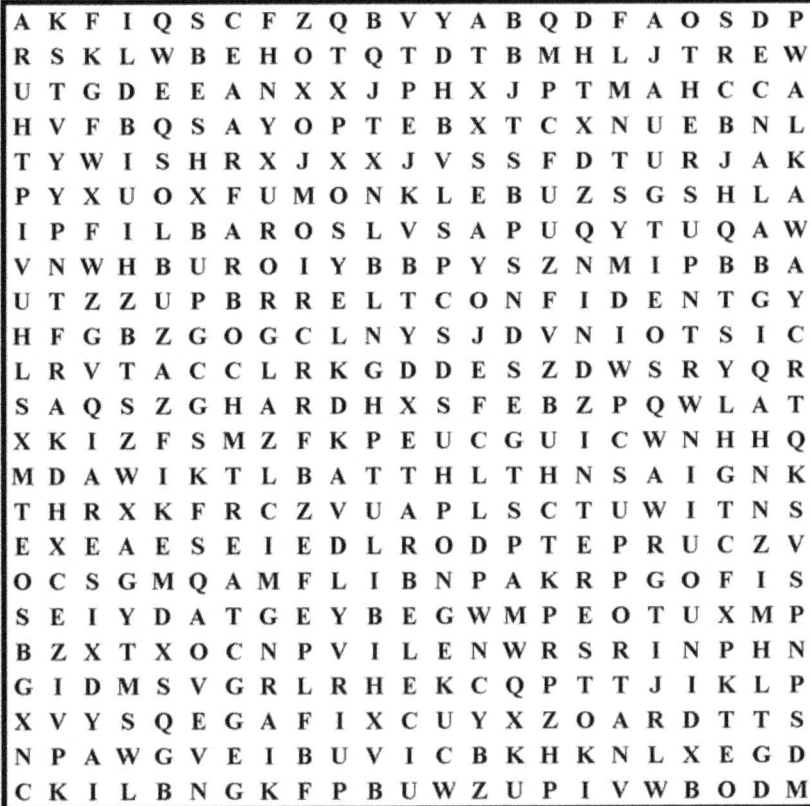

```
A K F I Q S C F Z Q B V Y A B Q D F A O S D P
R S K L W B E H O T Q T D T B M H L J T R E W
U T G D E E A N X X J P H X J P T M A H C C A
H V F B Q S A Y O P T E B X T C X N U E B N L
T Y W I S H R X J X X J V S S F D T U R J A K
P Y X U O X F U M O N K L E B U Z S G S H L A
I P F I L B A R O S L V S A P U Q Y T U Q A W
V N W H B U R O I Y B B P Y S Z N M I P B B A
U T Z Z U P B R R E L T C O N F I D E N T G Y
H F G B Z G O G C L N Y S J D V N I O T S I C
L R V T A C C L R K G D D E S Z D W S R Y Q R
S A Q S Z G H A R D H X S F E B Z P Q W L A T
X K I Z F S M Z F K P E U C G U I C W N H H Q
M D A W I K T L B A T T H L T H N S A I G N K
T H R X K F R C Z V U A P L S C T U W I T N S
E X E A E S E I E D L R O D P T E P R U C Z V
O C S G M Q A M F L I B N P A K R P G O F I S
S E I Y D A T G E Y B E G W M P E O T U X M P
B Z X T X O C N P V I L E N W R S R I N P H N
G I D M S V G R L R H E K C Q P T T J I K L P
X V Y S Q E G A F I X C U Y X Z O A R D T T S
N P A W G V E I B U V I C B K H K N L X E G D
C K I L B N G K F P B U W Z U P I V W B O D M
```

balanced	friends	standup
celebrate	friendships	support
challenge	interest	treat
confident	others	walkaway
drama	right	yourself

Chapter 3

How to Handle Disagreements in the Sixth Grade Classroom

Hey there, sixth-grade problem solver! Disagreements are a normal part of life, and in sixth grade, they can happen more often. Maybe someone has a different idea for a group project, or you and a friend disagree about the rules of a game during recess. Learning how to handle disagreements the right way can help you avoid drama, build stronger relationships, and make your classroom a better place for everyone. In this chapter, we'll explore tips, strategies, and real-life sixth-grade scenarios to help you handle conflicts like a pro. Let's dive in!

1. Stay Calm—Even If You're Frustrated

The first step in solving any disagreement is keeping your cool. If you get angry or upset, it's harder to think clearly. Take a deep breath and count to five before you say anything.

Real-Life Scenario:
You're working on a group poster for science, and one teammate keeps ignoring your ideas. You feel your frustration building, but instead of yelling, you take a deep breath and say calmly, "Can we talk about everyone's ideas? I want to make sure we're all included."

2. Use "I" Statements to Express Yourself

In sixth grade, you're learning to communicate like a leader. When you have a disagreement, avoid blaming others. Instead, use "I" statements to explain how you feel.

Real-Life Scenario:
You think a classmate cut in line for the water fountain. Instead of saying, "You're always cutting in line!" you say, "I feel frustrated when people cut in line because we're all waiting our turn." This keeps the focus on the problem, not the person.

3. Listen to Their Side of the Story
Disagreements are rarely one-sided. Taking the time to listen to the other person may change your perspective.

Real-Life Scenario:
You and a friend are arguing about who should present first during your history project. When you ask why they want to go first, they say, "I get really nervous, and I'd rather just get it over with." Now you understand their feelings and decide to let them go first.

4. Find a Compromise
In sixth grade, finding a middle ground can often solve disagreements. Look for a solution that works for both sides.

Real-Life Scenario:
During art class, you and your partner disagree on which colors to use for your painting. You want bright colors, and they want earth tones. You suggest using both: bright colors for the background and earth tones for the foreground. Problem solved!

5. Take Responsibility for Your Part
If you've done something to contribute to the disagreement, own up to it. Taking responsibility shows maturity and helps fix the situation faster.

Real-Life Scenario:
You interrupt your classmate during a group discussion, and they snap, "Can I finish my sentence?" Instead of arguing, you say, "You're right—I shouldn't have interrupted. Go ahead." The tension disappears, and the group moves on.

6. Ask a Teacher for Help (When Needed)
Sometimes, disagreements get too big to handle on your own. If you've tried to solve the problem and it's not working, ask a teacher or another adult for help.

Real-Life Scenario:
A classmate keeps making mean jokes about your work during group projects, and they won't stop even when you ask them to. You tell your teacher, who talks to the classmate privately. The jokes stop, and you feel relieved.

7. Avoid Gossiping
Talking behind someone's back might feel like a quick way to vent, but it usually makes things worse. Instead of gossiping, focus on solving the problem directly.

Real-Life Scenario:
You're upset because a friend didn't invite you to their lunch table. Instead of complaining to other classmates, you talk to your friend privately and say, "I felt left out when I couldn't sit with you. Can we talk about it?" They apologize, and you work things out.

8. Know When to Walk Away
Not every disagreement needs to be solved right away. If emotions are running high, take a break and come back to the conversation later when you're both calmer.

Real-Life Scenario:
You and a classmate are arguing about how to solve a math problem. They start raising their voice, and you feel yourself getting frustrated. You say, "Let's take a break first, then finish this problem." Later, you both feel calmer and work together to solve the problem.

9. Be Open to Different Perspectives

In sixth grade, you're learning that not everyone thinks the same way you do—and that's okay. Try to see the disagreement from the other person's perspective.

Real-Life Scenario:

You and a friend argue about which book to read for your group project. You want something exciting, but they suggest a classic. After hearing their reasons (it's easier to find information about the classic), you realize their idea makes sense.

10. Celebrate the Solution

When you work through a disagreement successfully, take a moment to appreciate what you accomplished. Solving conflicts builds stronger relationships and shows how much you've grown.

Real-Life Scenario:

You and a classmate argue over who should write the final draft of your group report. After talking it out, you decide to split the work—you'll write the introduction, and they'll write the conclusion. When you finish the project, you high-five and feel proud of how you worked together.

11. Learn From the Experience

Every disagreement is a chance to learn something new about yourself and others. Think about what worked, what didn't, and how you can handle similar situations in the future.

Real-Life Scenario:

You realize that interrupting people often leads to arguments. After a disagreement with a friend, you decide to practice waiting your turn to speak. Over time, your conversations become smoother, and your friends notice your effort.

Final Thought

Disagreements in sixth grade don't have to turn into arguments or drama. By staying calm, listening, and working together to find solutions, you can handle conflicts in a way that strengthens your friendships and makes your classroom a better place. Remember, solving disagreements isn't about "winning"—it's about understanding and respecting each other. So the next time a disagreement pops up, take a deep breath, use these tips, and show everyone how mature and awesome you are. You've got this, sixth grader!

```
O W Y J W G J E O A P G A K E O R S G Y K E P
T E I F S M O T S S Q S J M S A Y K O W F R U
G X C X T A H I Q Y G N V F I W D K D Q C G S
C D V K N H Q S J Q H X S U M I J A Q I O W E
H G U P E G A T H A H M N G O S S I P I N G V
Q B U X M A A A R U K A R K R O Z E Z J F M I
Y W N Z E M A T I R E T L A P L D F I U L K T
X H C S E R F E Q L Y U S V M U W L W Z I F C
J E M Z R P Y M M S Q R S V O T W R O S C Y E
M P Q S G S X E S X V E H A C I D J Z I T Z P
L M Z S A F M N Y J R O C Q X O F Q H I S F S
E Z G P S G O T P C W A W Q I N T H L U W M R
C J G I I N U S I H L O C P L X B I G R B I E
N X C H D G P R H M J V Y E M M B Z N S K S P
E F I S M H Y H T L E I J G G I E H B G Y P E
I Q A N Q A B A H K T S F K S B X L D K C H F
R E D O L C L O V N N L D N B K H I Z W C H Q
E Z J I K O F X Y G T P O T C L A S S R O O M
P P K T R N C D M K C P X M Q V C T P B F M R
X Y C A L A P B K T S O J H T A K E I H E L P
E H M L S D R U H E N L M U Q M A N V M E J Z
J X L E R N H N R O M E Q C B Z P I B S Q Q U
U F I R D W P O S G A J H Q W A U C B O U G A
```

calm	experience	listen
classroom	gossiping	mature
compromise	help	perspectives
conflicts	istatements	relationships
disagreements	(I statements)	responsibility
		solution

Chapter 4

How to Handle Disagreements Outside the Sixth-Grade Classroom

Hey there, sixth-grade peacemaker! Life outside the classroom can be full of fun—recess games, lunchroom chats, after-school hangouts, and sports practice. But let's be honest: disagreements happen, even in these fun places. Maybe someone doesn't agree with the rules of a game, or there's an argument about who gets to sit where at lunch. Whatever the situation, handling disagreements the right way can save the day and even make your friendships stronger. In this chapter, we'll explore tons of tips, strategies, and real-life sixth-grade scenarios to help you handle conflicts like a pro.

1. Stay Cool and Think First

When a disagreement starts, it's easy to let your emotions take over. But staying calm is the best way to keep the situation from getting worse. Pause, take a deep breath, and think about what you really want to say before responding.

Real-Life Scenario:

You're playing basketball at recess, and someone keeps calling fouls that you don't think are fair. Instead of shouting, "You're wrong!" and causing a scene, you take a deep breath and say, "Can we talk about what counts as a foul before we keep playing?"

2. Use Humor to Break the Tension

Sometimes, a little humor can help everyone relax and see that the disagreement isn't such a big deal. Just make sure your joke isn't aimed at anyone involved.

Real-Life Scenario:
At lunch, you and your friend argue about who gets the last chocolate milk. You laugh and say, "Let's arm-wrestle for it—winner takes the milk!" Everyone laughs, and you end up splitting the milk instead of arguing about it.

3. Set Clear Rules for Games
Most playground or recess disagreements start because people don't agree on the rules. Before you start playing, make sure everyone understands how the game will work.

Real-Life Scenario:
Your group wants to play dodgeball, but half the players think catching the ball doesn't count as an out. You say, "Let's vote on the rules before we start so we're all on the same page." Once the rules are clear, the game goes smoothly.

4. Stand Up for What's Fair
Don't be afraid to speak up if someone is receiving unfair treatment. Being a good friend means making sure everyone gets a fair chance, even if it's not always easy.

Real-Life Scenario:
During soccer practice, one teammate keeps hogging the ball and not passing to others. You say, "Hey, we're a team—we all need a chance to practice." The teammate listens, and the game becomes more balanced.

5. Walk Away When It's Not Worth It
Sometimes, the best way to handle a disagreement is to simply walk away. Not every argument needs to be solved, especially if it's about something small.

Real-Life Scenario:
You and a friend are arguing about which movie to watch at a sleepover. As the argument heats up, you suggest taking a break and discussing it later. After playing a board game together, you both feel calmer and agree on a movie.

6. Listen to the Other Person's Point of View
In sixth grade, disagreements often happen because people don't feel heard. Try listening to the other person—it may change your perspective.

Real-Life Scenario:
You and your friend argue about who should get to sit next to your other friend on the bus. When you listen, your friend says they've had a rough day and just want some extra support. You realize it's not about the seat, and you offer to let them sit there.

7. Avoid "He Said, She Said" Drama
When disagreements involve more than two people, it's easy for things to spiral into gossip or finger-pointing. Focus on solving the problem directly, not dragging other people into it.

Real-Life Scenario:
Your group of friends is arguing about who was supposed to bring snacks to a club meeting. Instead of blaming someone, you say, "Let's all bring snacks next time so this doesn't happen again." The problem gets solved without creating more drama.

8. Apologize When You Need To
If you realize you've made a mistake or hurt someone's feelings, don't be afraid to say sorry. A sincere apology can fix a lot of problems.

Real-Life Scenario:
You tease a friend during a game, and they get upset. You say, "I'm sorry—I didn't mean to hurt your feelings." They forgive you, and you both move on.

9. Find a Compromise
Compromising means meeting in the middle so everyone feels like they've been heard. It's a great way to solve disagreements when both sides have valid points.

Real-Life Scenario:
You and your sibling are arguing about who gets to play the new video game first. You agree to let them go first this time, and you'll go first next time. Problem solved!

10. Know When to Ask for Help
If a disagreement is getting too big or someone is being mean, it's okay to ask an adult for help. Teachers, parents, or coaches can help you find a solution.

Real-Life Scenario:
A classmate keeps cutting in line at the water fountain, and they won't listen when you ask them to stop. You tell a teacher, who talks to them privately. The problem stops, and you feel relieved.

11. Learn to Let Go
Not every disagreement needs to end with someone being "right." Sometimes, the best way to maintain peace is to let go and move on.

Real-Life Scenario:
You and a friend argue about which team won in kickball. You realize it's not worth fighting over and say, "Let's just call it a tie." Your friend agrees, and you both move on to the next game.

Final Thought

Disagreements outside the classroom don't have to ruin your day. By staying calm, listening, and working toward fair solutions, you can handle conflicts in a way that makes everyone feel respected. Remember, solving disagreements isn't about winning—it's about keeping things fun and building stronger friendships. So the next time a disagreement pops up, try these tips and show everyone how mature and awesome you are. You've got this, sixth grader!

Chapter 4 How to Handle Disagreements Outside the Sixth Grade Classroom

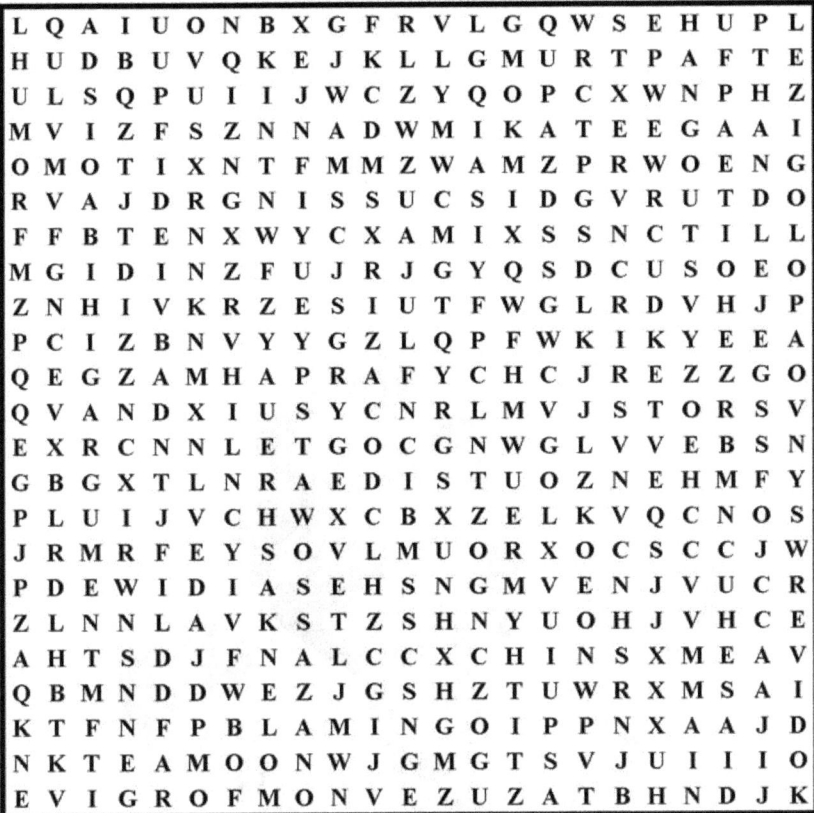

```
L Q A I U O N B X G F R V L G Q W S E H U P L
H U D B U V Q K E J K L L G M U R T P A F T E
U L S Q P U I I J W C Z Y Q O P C X W N P H Z
M V I Z F S Z N N A D W M I K A T E E G A A I
O M O T I X N T F M M Z W A M Z P R W O E N G
R V A J D R G N I S S U C S I D G V R U T D O
F F B T E N X W Y C X A M I X S S N C T I L L
M G I D I N Z F U J R J G Y Q S D C U S O E O
Z N H I V K R Z E S I U T F W G L R D V H J P
P C I Z B N V Y Y G Z L Q P F W K I K Y E E A
Q E G Z A M H A P R A F Y C H C J R E Z Z G O
Q V A N D X I U S Y C N R L M V J S T O R S V
E X R C N N L E T G O C G N W G L V V E B S N
G B G X T L N R A E D I S T U O Z N E H M F Y
P L U I J V C H W X C B X Z E L K V Q C N O S
J R M R F E Y S O V L M U O R X O C S C C J W
P D E W I D I A S E H S N G M V E N J V U C R
Z L N N L A V K S T Z S H N Y U O H J V H C E
A H T S D J F N A L C C X C H I N S X M E A V
Q B M N D D W E Z J G S H Z T U W R X M S A I
K T F N F P B L A M I N G O I P P N X A A J D
N K T E A M O O N W J G M G T S V J U I I I O
E V I G R O F M O N V E Z U Z A T B H N D J K
```

agree / emotions / he said (he said)
apologize / fair / humor
argument / forgive / letgo (let go)
blaming / handle / outside
discussing / hangouts / she said (she said)

37

Chapter 5

How to Ask Good Questions in the Sixth-Grade Classroom

Hey there, sixth-grade thinker! Asking good questions is one of the most powerful tools you have in the classroom. In sixth grade, your questions can show you're paying attention, help you understand tricky topics, and even make you look like a leader. Not all questions are created equal. Some can spark amazing conversations, while others might not get the answers you need. So how do you ask the right questions? This chapter is packed with tips, ideas, and real-life sixth-grade scenarios to help you level up your questioning skills. Let's get started!

1. Know When to Ask

Timing is everything. The middle of a lecture might not be the best time to ask about your homework from last week. Pay attention to when your teacher pauses, asks for questions, or looks like they're waiting for you to jump in.

Real-Life Scenario:

Your math teacher is explaining fractions, but you don't understand how to simplify them. Instead of interrupting mid-sentence, you wait until they ask, "Does anyone have questions about this step?" You raise your hand and ask, and the teacher explains it in a way that finally makes sense.

2. Make It Specific

Broad questions like "Can you explain that again?" might not get you the answer you need. Instead, be specific about what's confusing you.

Real-Life Scenario:
During a history lesson, the teacher mentions "the Industrial Revolution." Instead of asking, "What's that?" you ask, "What made the Industrial Revolution different from earlier time periods?" This helps you get a clear, detailed answer.

3. Connect It to What You Already Know
Good questions often come from linking new information to something you've already learned. This shows your teacher that you're making connections—and helps you understand the material better.

Real-Life Scenario:
Your science teacher is talking about energy transfer in ecosystems. You raise your hand and ask, "Is this like the food chain we studied last year, where energy moves from plants to animals?" Your teacher nods and expands on the idea, making it easier for you to understand.

4. Be Curious, Not Afraid
Some students worry that asking questions will make them look silly. Here's the truth: Asking questions shows you're paying attention and care about learning. Teachers love when you're curious!

Real-Life Scenario:
In English class, you're not sure what "foreshadowing" means. You raise your hand and ask, "Can you give another example of foreshadowing in this story?" Your teacher smiles and says, "Great question!" before giving a clearer example.

5. Use Open-Ended Questions

Open-ended questions start with "how," "why," or "what if" and lead to longer, more detailed answers. These questions can spark excellent discussions and help you dive deeper into the topic.

Real-Life Scenario:

Your social studies teacher is talking about ancient civilizations. Instead of asking, "Did they use money?" you ask, "How did people trade goods before money was invented?" This opens the door to a bigger explanation about bartering and early economies.

6. Practice Active Listening

If you're paying close attention, you might sometimes already have the answers to your questions. Pay close attention during lessons and discussions to prevent the repetition of previously explained information.

Real-Life Scenario:

Your science teacher says, "The Earth's rotation causes day and night." You almost ask, "What causes night?" but catch yourself because the answer was just explained. Instead, you ask, "Does the speed of Earth's rotation ever change?" and learn something even cooler.

7. Follow Up with Another Question

When your teacher answers your first question, think of a follow-up to dig deeper. This shows you're engaged and helps you explore the topic more fully.

Real-Life Scenario:
In math, you ask, "Why do we use variables in algebra?" After your teacher explains, you follow up with, "How do you know what number a variable stands for?" Now you've turned one question into two answers!

8. Write Down Your Questions
Sometimes, you think of a great question but forget it by the time the teacher pauses. Keep a notebook handy to jot down your questions as they come to you.

Real-Life Scenario:
During a reading assignment, you wonder, "Why did the author choose this setting?" You write it in your notebook, then ask it during the class discussion. Your teacher praises you for paying attention to the details.

9. Ask About Real-Life Applications
A great way to make learning meaningful is to ask how it connects to the real world. Teachers love explaining how what you're learning can be useful outside the classroom.

Real-Life Scenario:
In math class, you're learning about percentages. You ask, "How are percentages used in real life?" Your teacher explains how they're used in sales, tips, and sports stats. Suddenly, percentages seem a lot more interesting!

10. Ask Questions That Help the Whole Class
If you're confused, chances are someone else is too. Don't be afraid to ask questions that might benefit your classmates as well.

Real-Life Scenario:
Your teacher assigns a group project but doesn't explain how long the presentation should be. You ask, "How many minutes should our presentation be?" Your classmates thank you later for clearing it up.

11. Learn the Art of Clarifying Questions
If something doesn't make sense, ask a question to clarify. Instead of saying, "I don't get it," say, "Can you explain the part about...?" This helps you get the exact information you need.

Real-Life Scenario:
In geography, your teacher talks about climate zones, but you're confused about the difference between "tropical" and "temperate." You ask, "Can you explain how tropical and temperate zones are different?" and finally understand.

12. Reflect on Your Questions
After class, think about the questions you asked. Did they help you understand better? How could you ask even better questions next time?

Real-Life Scenario:
You asked your science teacher about renewable energy but realized your question was too vague. Next time, you plan to ask, "What makes solar energy more sustainable than fossil fuels?"

Final Thought

Asking good questions in sixth grade isn't just about getting answers —it's about learning how to think critically, connect ideas, and explore new possibilities. The better your questions, the more you'll get out of your classes. So next time you're curious or confused, don't be afraid to raise your hand. Your questions could spark excellent conversations, impress your teacher, and even inspire your classmates. You've got this, sixth-grade thinker!

Chapter 5 How to Ask Good Questions in the Sixth Grade Classroom

```
D E A O B B F N C S E U A W J E Y F I R A L C
U Q J P X X W E E V D E D N E N E P O I V U X
O D A U A F E N I T C A U X Y M H C F T K X X
Y M Y W T O B T T Z T B N Z W U R H I L S B B
S S F O T R C G J Q I I X U W E A P R Z Z D L
R L X L E A I J Q G Y E F D A I H M N L S D I
C K H L N V S K P E R S E L S M D B R B R U S
F L I O T U C O P Z L H W B Q N G I I U E I T
C C I F I C E P S V F O Z P H J O X W R W V E
H D B A O I P Z R P R L X C E A P I R F S G N
Y B T E N G F A U L B C I K E V K V T Q N X I
G H E Q K X O W D F Q J W Z R N G K Y S A N N
B C I Q I W F G Y R M U X X Y P Y N U P E D G
V F P A H T Y B W O O X X U Z Z B O V G Y U T
Y C V A Z A C P R S A H F M D S H I J W L U Q
T U L G L J E E S L W Y A M E L W T K T B C S
Z R M U F O K V L C V A T S A R O A J P Y O G
H I G J Y U X G R F A O J V C F Q M Z M C A N
C O N N E C T D R T E E A Y Y I H R G J B K A
Y U Y L B I N B T Q B R C V I A R O N V W P E
D S X Q G H Y S H W I A L Z X I D F M R L H K
O U D W E M S O N N F M O X V S B N E R B D F
O G Z P N W P O W E R F U L M V J I O V A F O
```

active	curious	powerful
answers	followup (follow up)	questions
attention	information	realworld (real world)
clarify	listening	reflect
connect	openended (open ended)	specific

Chapter 6

How to Work Collaboratively in Small Groups in Sixth Grade

Hey there, teamwork champ! In sixth grade, working in small groups is a big deal. Whether you're creating a science experiment, brainstorming for a class presentation, or solving a math problem, teamwork is everywhere. But let's be real—group work can sometimes be frustrating. People don't always agree, and not everyone puts in the same effort. The good news? With the right strategies, you can make group work smooth, successful, and even fun. This chapter is packed with tips, real-life scenarios, and ideas to help you crush small group work in sixth grade. Let's get started!

1. Start With a Game Plan
Before jumping into the assignment, take a few minutes to discuss your group's goals and how you'll achieve them. A clear plan keeps everyone on the same page and avoids confusion later.

Real-Life Scenario:
You're assigned a group project on renewable energy. Instead of arguing over who does what, you suggest, "Let's write down all the tasks we need to do and then divide them up." Your group lists research, visuals, and presenting. Once the tasks are assigned, everyone knows what they're responsible for.

2. Communicate Clearly and Respectfully
Good communication is the heart of teamwork. Share your ideas, but also listen to others. Speak respectfully, even if you don't agree with someone's suggestion.

Real-Life Scenario:
During a history project, one teammate suggests a creative (but complicated) idea for your presentation. Instead of saying, "That's a terrible idea," you say, "I like where you're going, but maybe we can simplify it so we have time to finish everything." Your teammate feels heard, and you move forward with a solid plan.

3. Play to Everyone's Strengths
In sixth grade, everyone has unique talents. Maybe one person is excellent at drawing, another is a strong writer, and someone else loves public speaking. Use those strengths to your group's advantage.

Real-Life Scenario:
Your group is creating a video for an English project. You're great at editing videos, so you volunteer to handle that part. Another classmate loves acting and takes the lead role, while a quieter teammate helps write the script. By dividing tasks based on strengths, your group creates an awesome project.

4. Stay Focused and On Task
If everyone is chatting or daydreaming, group work can easily get off track. Set small goals for each part of the assignment to stay on track.

Real-Life Scenario:
You're building a model of a volcano for science, but half your group is talking about the latest video game. You say, "Let's finish painting the volcano first, and then we can chat while it dries." Everyone agrees, and you get back on track.

5. Handle Disagreements Like a Pro

Disagreements are normal in group work, but how you handle them makes all the difference. Stay calm, listen to each other, and find a compromise that works for everyone.

Real-Life Scenario:

Your group can't agree on the title for a history presentation. You suggest, "How about we each write down our favorite title and vote on it?" After voting, the group chooses the most popular option and moves forward.

6. Make Sure Everyone Contributes

In sixth grade, teamwork means everyone should pitch in. If someone isn't doing their part, encourage them to get involved without being bossy.

Real-Life Scenario:

One teammate hasn't done much for your geography project. You say, "Hey, we still need to label the map and add captions. Do you want to take charge of that?" They agree, and now the workload feels fair.

7. Use Tools to Stay Organized

Staying organized is key to a successful project. Use tools like shared documents, checklists, or timelines to keep track of your progress.

Real-Life Scenario:

Your group uses a shared online document to work on a science report. Everyone can see what's done and what still needs work. When your teacher asks for a progress update, you easily show how far along you are.

8. Respect Deadlines

In sixth grade, teachers expect you to manage your time wisely. Make sure your group sets smaller deadlines for each part of the project so everything gets done on time.

Real-Life Scenario:
Your group sets a deadline to finish the research section of your project by Wednesday, so there's time to work on visuals and practice presenting. When Wednesday comes, you're all on track and stress-free.

9. Keep a Positive Attitude

Teamwork isn't always easy, but staying positive helps keep everyone motivated. Encourage your teammates and focus on the goal, not the challenges.

Real-Life Scenario:
Your group's first draft of a class play doesn't go well, and everyone feels discouraged. You say, "It's okay—this is just the first step. Let's brainstorm ways to make it better." Your optimism helps the group bounce back and come up with a great final version.

10. Give Credit Where It's Due

Celebrate everyone's hard work at the end of the project. Acknowledging each person's contribution makes the group feel proud and appreciated.

Real-Life Scenario:
After presenting your group's climate change poster, you say, "Great job, everyone! The visuals you created looked amazing, and your explanation of the solutions was really clear." Your teammates smile, and you all feel good about the effort you put in.

11. Glows and Grows

After the project is over, think about glows, what went well, and grows—what could be improved. This helps you get even better at group work next time.

Real-Life Scenario:

You realize that waiting until the last minute to create the slideshow caused a lot of stress. Next time, you plan to finish all visuals a day earlier to avoid the rush.

Final Thought

In sixth grade, group work is about more than just finishing a project —it's about learning how to collaborate, communicate, and solve problems together. By staying organized, respecting your teammates, and handling disagreements maturely, you'll become a pro at working with others. Plus, you'll create amazing projects that you're proud to share. So the next time your teacher says, "Get into groups," don't stress—use these tips, and show everyone what a sixth-grade teamwork star looks like. Let's go!

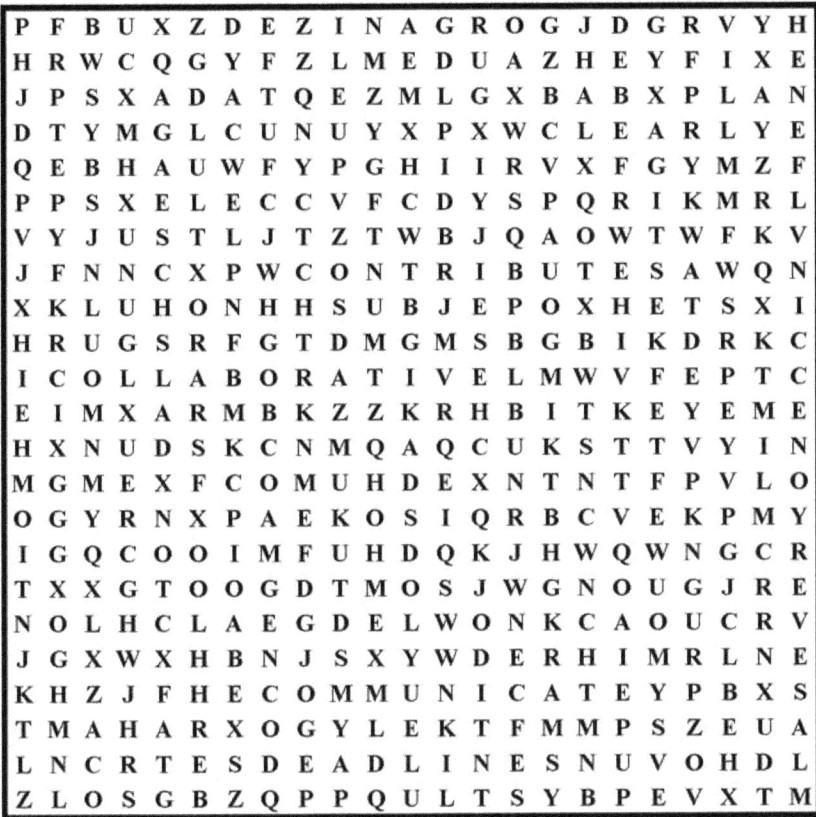

```
P F B U X Z D E Z I N A G R O G J D G R V Y H
H R W C Q G Y F Z L M E D U A Z H E Y F I X E
J P S X A D A T Q E Z M L G X B A B X P L A N
D T Y M G L C U N U Y X P X W C L E A R L Y E
Q E B H A U W F Y P G H I I R V X F G Y M Z F
P P S X E L E C C V F C D Y S P Q R I K M R L
V Y J U S T L J T Z T W B J Q A O W T W F K V
J F N N C X P W C O N T R I B U T E S A W Q N
X K L U H O N H H S U B J E P O X H E T S X I
H R U G S R F G T D M G M S B G B I K D R K C
I C O L L A B O R A T I V E L M W V F E P T C
E I M X A R M B K Z Z K R H B I T K E Y E M E
H X N U D S K C N M Q A Q C U K S T T V Y I N
M G M E X F C O M U H D E X N T N T F P V L O
O G Y R N X P A E K O S I Q R B C V E K P M Y
I G Q C O O I M F U H D Q K J H W Q W N G C R
T X X G T O O G D T M O S J W G N O U G J R E
N O L H C L A E G D E L W O N K C A O U C R V
J G X W X H B N J S X Y W D E R H I M R L N E
K H Z J F H E C O M M U N I C A T E Y P B X S
T M A H A R X O G Y L E K T F M M P S Z E U A
L N C R T E S D E A D L I N E S N U V O H D L
Z L O S G B Z Q P P Q U L T S Y B P E V X T M
```

acknowledge	deadlines	organized
clearly	everyone	plan
collaborative	focused	small
communicate	groups	strengths
contributes	listen	task

54

Chapter 7

How to Succeed in Studying History in Sixth Grade

Hey there, sixth-grade historian! History isn't just a bunch of dates and names—it's the story of how people, places, and events shaped the world we live in today. In sixth grade, history takes on a whole new level. You're not just learning about what happened—you're digging deeper into why it happened and how everything connects. Ready to unlock the secrets of the past and become a history pro? Let's dive into tons of tips, real-life scenarios, and ideas to help you rock sixth-grade history!

1. Connect the Past to Your World

History becomes more fascinating when you see how it connects to your life today. Ask yourself: How does this event or person relate to the world I live in?

Real-Life Scenario:

You're learning about the ancient Greeks, and your teacher talks about democracy. You realize that the system of voting in ancient Athens is similar to how elections work in modern democracies. Suddenly, ancient Greece feels more relevant, and you can explain why it matters in class discussions.

2. Create a Timeline

History often feels overwhelming because there's so much to remember. A timeline helps you see how events fit together and which ones happened at the same time.

Real-Life Scenario:
Your class is studying World War II, and you're struggling to remember all the events. You create a timeline showing key moments, like when the war started, when major battles occurred, and when it ended. When your teacher asks about D-Day, you can confidently place it in 1944 because it's right there on your timeline.

3. Take Notes Like a Detective
Great historians don't just copy what they read—they hunt for the most important clues. As you read or listen to lessons, jot down key facts, causes, and effects.

Real-Life Scenario:
Your teacher gives a lecture on the Industrial Revolution. Instead of writing everything down, you focus on main ideas like "machines replaced hand tools" and "factories grew near rivers." When it's time to study, your notes are clear and simple to review.

4. Dive Into Primary Sources
Primary sources—like letters, diaries, or speeches from the time period you're studying—give you a firsthand look at history. They help you understand how people felt and thought back then.

Real-Life Scenario:
You're studying Abraham Lincoln, and your teacher shows the Gettysburg Address. Reading his actual words about freedom and equality makes his speech more powerful than just reading about it in your textbook.

5. Ask "Why" and "How" Questions

History isn't just about what happened—it's about why it happened and how it shaped the future. Asking deeper questions helps you understand the big picture.

Real-Life Scenario:

When studying the fall of the Roman Empire, you ask, "Why did Rome weaken over time?" Your teacher explains how invasions, economic troubles, and poor leadership all played a role. Now, you can explain the reasons in detail.

6. Use Visuals to Understand

Maps, charts, and diagrams are your best friends in history class. They help you see where things happened and how they're connected.

Real-Life Scenario:

You're studying the Silk Road, but the idea of trade routes across Asia feels confusing. Then, your teacher shows a map with arrows marking the paths. Suddenly, you can picture how goods like silk and spices traveled from one place to another.

7. Compare and Contrast

When studying different civilizations, leaders, or events, look for similarities and differences. This helps you see patterns and understand history on a deeper level.

Real-Life Scenario:

Your teacher asks how the American and French Revolutions are similar and different. You realize both fought for freedom, but the American Revolution focused on independence from Britain, while the French Revolution was about overthrowing the monarchy. Your answer stands out because you see both sides.

8. Make History Fun with Stories

Every historical figure and event has a story. Instead of memorizing facts, think about history as a series of exciting (and sometimes dramatic) tales.

Real-Life Scenario:

Instead of just remembering "Alexander the Great conquered Persia," imagine him leading his army through deserts, facing massive battles, and becoming a legend. When you picture history as a movie in your head, it's easier to remember.

9. Use Technology to Explore More

Videos, online simulations, and history apps can bring the past to life. Use these tools to go beyond the textbook and dive deeper into topics that interest you.

Real-Life Scenario:

You're learning about ancient Egypt, and your teacher shows a virtual tour of the Great Pyramid. Seeing how it was built and what's inside makes the lesson unforgettable. Later, you ace a quiz because you can picture everything you learned.

10. Work with Your Classmates

Teamwork makes history even more interesting. Share ideas, debate different viewpoints, and help each other understand tricky topics.

Real-Life Scenario:

The Renaissance is the topic of your group's project. You take charge of researching Leonardo da Vinci, while your classmates cover Michelangelo and the printing press. When you put it all together, your presentation is amazing because everyone contributed.

11. Practice for Tests with "Why" Questions

When studying for a history test, focus on understanding why things happened, not just memorizing dates. Use your notes to write practice questions and quiz yourself.

Real-Life Scenario:

You write, "Why did the American colonies declare independence from Britain?" You answer: "Because of unfair taxes and lack of representation in government." When this question appears on the exam, you will be prepared.

12. Learn from Mistakes

Not every answer will be perfect, and that's okay. Look at your mistakes to understand where you went wrong and how to improve.

Real-Life Scenario:

You mix up the Civil War and Revolutionary War on a quiz. Your teacher explains how they're different, and you create a chart comparing the two. By the next test, you've got it down.

13. Share What You've Learned

One of the best ways to remember history is to teach it to someone else. Share your new knowledge with friends or family.

Real-Life Scenario:

At dinner, you tell your family about how the Great Wall of China was built to protect against invasions. They ask questions, and explaining the story helps you remember the details for your next history discussion in class.

Final Thought

Studying history in sixth grade is about more than just memorizing facts—it's about exploring stories, asking questions, and understanding how the past shapes the present. With these tips, you'll not only ace your history class but also learn skills that will stay with you for life. So grab your textbook, open your notebook, and dive into the incredible adventure of history. You've got this, sixth-grade historian!

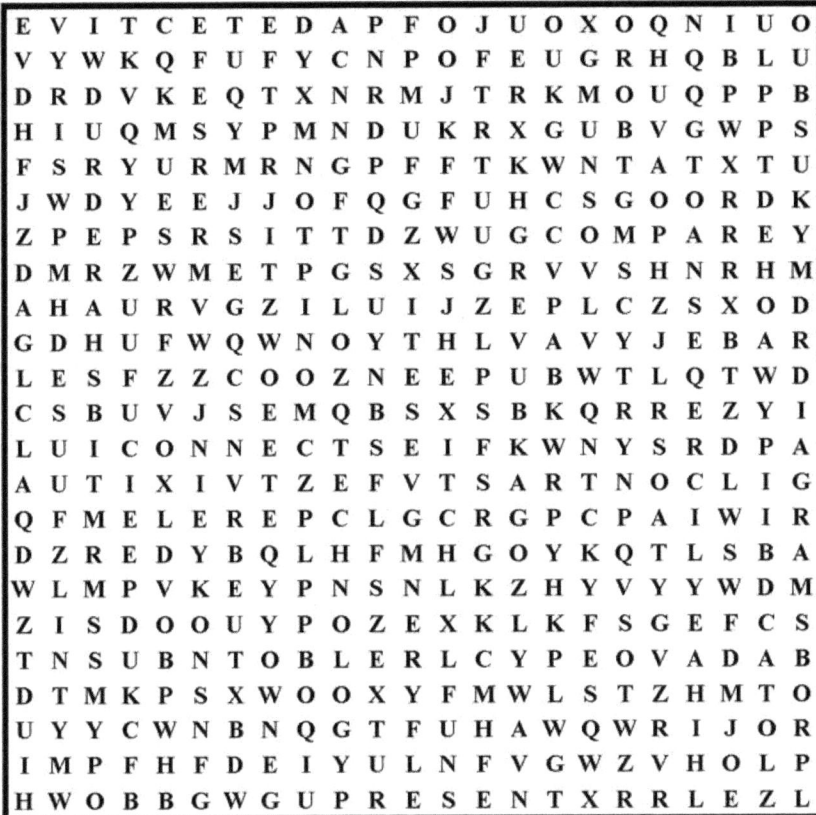

```
E V I T C E T E D A P F O J U O X O Q N I U O
V Y W K Q F U F Y C N P O F E U G R H Q B L U
D R D V K E Q T X N R M J T R K M O U Q P P B
H I U Q M S Y P M N D U K R X G U B V G W P S
F S R Y U R M R N G P F F T K W N T A T X T U
J W D Y E E J J O F Q G F U H C S G O O R D K
Z P E P S R S I T T D Z W U G C O M P A R E Y
D M R Z W M E T P G S X S G R V V S H N R H M
A H A U R V G Z I L U I J Z E P L C Z S X O D
G D H U F W Q W N O Y T H L V A V Y J E B A R
L E S F Z Z C O O Z N E E P U B W T L Q T W D
C S B U V J S E M Q B S X S B K Q R R E Z Y I
L U I C O N N E C T S E I F K W N Y S R D P A
A U T I X I V T Z E F V T S A R T N O C L I G
Q F M E L E R E P C L G C R G P C P A I W I R
D Z R E D Y B Q L H F M H G O Y K Q T L S B A
W L M P V K E Y P N S N L K Z H Y V Y Y W D M
Z I S D O O U Y P O Z E X K L K F S G E F C S
T N S U B N T O B L E R L C Y P E O V A D A B
D T M K P S X W O O X Y F M W L S T Z H M T O
U Y Y C W N B N Q G T F U H A W Q W R I J O R
I M P F H F D E I Y U L N F V G W Z V H O L P
H W O B B G W G U P R E S E N T X R R L E Z L
```

charts	detective	questions
compare	diagrams	share
connects	fun	technology
contrast	history	timeline
dates	present	visuals

Chapter 8

How to Succeed in Sixth Grade Math

Hey there, sixth-grade math wizard! Sixth grade math is where things get serious—and seriously exciting. You're diving into concepts like ratios, decimals, percentages, geometry, and maybe even a little pre-algebra. Don't let the big words scare you—this year is all about building on what you already know and learning how to tackle new challenges. In this chapter, you'll find tons of tips, strategies, and real-life sixth-grade scenarios to help you master math and feel confident in every class. Ready? Let's add some skills, subtract the stress, and multiply your confidence!

1. Understand the "Why" Behind the Math

In sixth grade, math isn't just about getting the answer—it's about understanding why things work the way they do. When you know the reason behind a formula or method, you'll find it easier to solve problems.

Real-Life Scenario:

Your teacher is explaining how to find the area of a triangle using the formula
Area = ½ × base × height. Instead of just memorizing it, you ask, "Why is it half the base times the height?" Your teacher shows you how a triangle is half of a rectangle, and now the formula makes perfect sense.

2. Stay Organized with Your Work

Keeping your math notes and assignments neat is more important than ever. Write clearly, use headings, and circle your final answers. This makes studying easier and helps you spot mistakes.

Real-Life Scenario:
You're solving a multi-step equation and accidentally drop a negative sign. Because your work is neat and easy to follow, you spot the mistake quickly and fix it before handing in your assignment.

3. Master Ratios and Proportions
Ratios and proportions pop up everywhere in sixth grade math, from recipes to maps to word problems. Practice setting up ratios and solving them step by step.

Real-Life Scenario:
Your class is making trail mix, and the recipe calls for a 2:3 ratio of peanuts to raisins. You want to make a bigger batch with 4 cups of peanuts. You set up a proportion:
$2/3 = 4/x$
and solve to find that you'll need 6 cups of raisins. Your snack turns out perfectly balanced!

4. Use Models and Visuals
Sometimes, drawing a picture or using a graph makes tricky problems easier to understand. Visualizing the problem can help you see the solution more clearly.

Real-Life Scenario:
You're solving a problem about dividing a pizza among 8 people. You draw a circle, slice it into 8 parts, and shade the slices to show each person's share. Seeing it drawn out helps you understand fractions better.

5. Practice Word Problems Like a Detective

Word problems can feel overwhelming, but breaking them down into smaller steps helps. Read carefully, underline key information, and write out what the problem is asking.

Real-Life Scenario:

The problem says, "A car travels 60 miles in 2 hours. How far will it go in 5 hours at the same speed?" You underline "60 miles in 2 hours" and figure out the rate: 30 miles per hour. Then you multiply $30 \times 5 = 150$. Now you've cracked the case!

6. Use Technology to Help

There are tons of apps and websites that make math more fun and interactive. Use them to practice tricky concepts or explore new ones.

Real-Life Scenario:

You're stuck on percentages, so your teacher suggests an online game where you solve percentage problems to build a virtual city. After playing for 15 minutes, you feel more confident about the topic —and your city looks awesome.

7. Don't Skip the Basics

Sixth grade math builds on everything you've learned so far, so make sure you're solid on multiplication, division, and fractions. These skills are like the foundation of a house—everything else depends on them.

Real-Life Scenario:

You're simplifying a fraction, and knowing your multiplication tables helps you quickly see that
36/48 can be reduced to 3/4. Your teacher notices your quick thinking and gives you a high-five.

8. Check Your Work (Twice!)
Even if you're confident in your answer, take a minute to double-check your work. Look for small mistakes, like forgetting a decimal or misplacing a negative sign.

Real-Life Scenario:
You finish a test and go back to check your work. You realize you accidentally wrote 5 instead of 0.5 in one answer. Fixing it earns you an extra point—and saves you from kicking yourself later.

9. Ask Questions That Go Deeper
If you're confused, don't hesitate to ask your teacher for help. Even better, ask questions that show you're thinking about the "big picture."

Real-Life Scenario:
Your teacher explains how to convert decimals to percentages by multiplying by 100. You ask, "Why does multiplying by 100 work?" Your teacher explains how percentages are based on parts of 100, and your understanding gets a major boost.

10. Learn to Estimate
Estimation is a superpower in math. It helps you quickly check if your answer makes sense and saves time on tests.

Real-Life Scenario:
You're solving 98×23, and your exact answer is 2,254. Before finishing, you estimate
$100 \times 20 = 2,000$, so you know your answer is in the right ballpark.

11. Turn Math into a Game
Studying doesn't have to be boring. Turn math into a challenge by racing the clock, competing with a friend, or turning problems into a game.

Real-Life Scenario:
You and your classmate challenge each other to solve equations as fast as possible. The winner gets bragging rights, and both of you get better at solving equations quickly.

12. Reflect on Your Mistakes
Mistakes are normal—they're how you learn. Look at where you went wrong and figure out how to avoid the same mistake next time.

Real-Life Scenario:
On a quiz, you forget the order of operations and get one problem wrong. Your teacher explains PEMDAS (Parentheses, Exponents, Multiplication, Division, Addition, and Subtraction), and you use it correctly on the next test.

13. Stay Persistent
Some math problems take time and effort to figure out. Don't give up —keep trying different strategies until you solve it.

Real-Life Scenario:
You're struggling with a tricky geometry problem, but instead of giving up, you draw a diagram, reread the question, and ask a friend for advice. When you finally solve it, it feels like a huge win.

Final Thought

Sixth grade math might feel challenging, but it's also full of opportunities to grow your skills and confidence. By staying organized, practicing regularly, and asking great questions, you'll tackle every topic that comes your way. So grab your pencil, sharpen your mind, and show sixth-grade math what you're made of. You've got this, math genius!

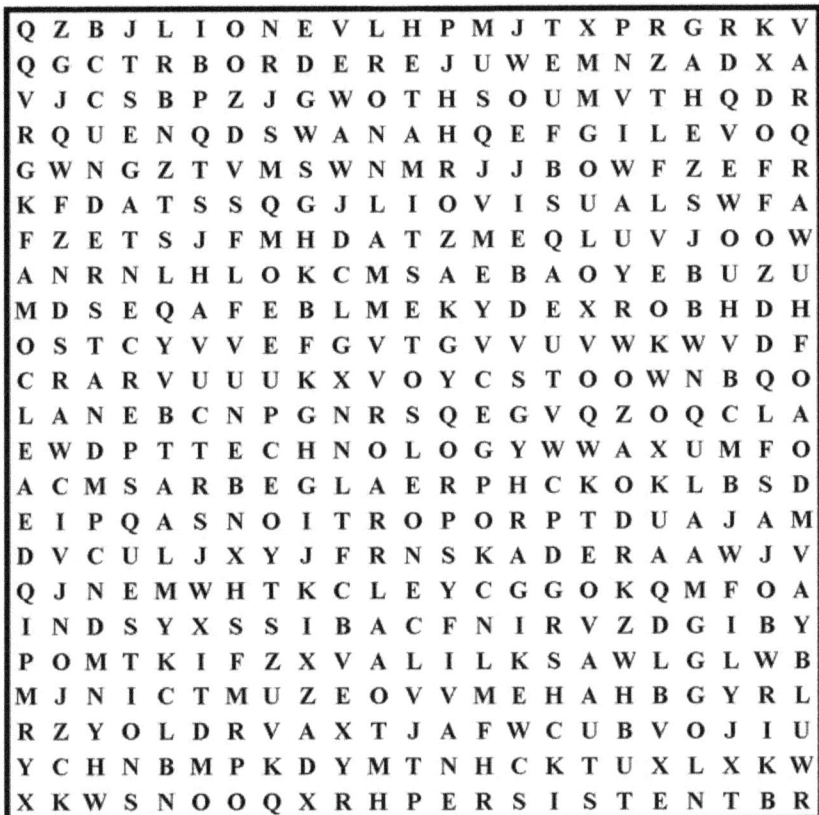

```
Q Z B J L I O N E V L H P M J T X P R G R K V
Q G C T R B O R D E R E J U W E M N Z A D X A
V J C S B P Z J G W O T H S O U M V T H Q D R
R Q U E N Q D S W A N A H Q E F G I L E V O Q
G W N G Z T V M S W N M R J J B O W F Z E F R
K F D A T S S Q G J L I O V I S U A L S W F A
F Z E T S J F M H D A T Z M E Q L U V J O O W
A N R N L H L O K C M S A E B A O Y E B U Z U
M D S E Q A F E B L M E K Y D E X R O B H D H
O S T C Y V V E F G V T G V V U V W K W V D F
C R A R V U U K X V O Y C S T O O W N B Q O
L A N E B C N P G N R S Q E G V Q Z O Q C L A
E W D P T T E C H N O L O G Y W W A X U M F O
A C M S A R B E G L A E R P H C K O K L B S D
E I P Q A S N O I T R O P O R P T D U A J A M
D V C U L J X Y J F R N S K A D E R A A W J V
Q J N E M W H T K C L E Y C G G O K Q M F O A
I N D S Y X S S I B A C F N I R V Z D G I B Y
P O M T K I F Z X V A L I L K S A W L G L W B
M J N I C T M U Z E O V V M E H A H B G Y R L
R Z Y O L D R V A X T J A F W C U B V O J I U
Y C H N B M P K D Y M T N H C K T U X L X K W
X K W S N O O Q X R H P E R S I S T E N T B R
```

basics	percentages	ratios
estimate	persistent	reflect
math	prealgebra	technology
models	proportions	understand
organized	questions	visuals

Chapter 9

How to Succeed in Reading in Sixth Grade

Welcome to sixth grade, future book lover! Reading in sixth grade is about more than just finishing a book—it's about thinking deeply, analyzing, and connecting stories to the world around you. You'll tackle novels, articles, poetry, and nonfiction texts that challenge you to think critically and stretch your imagination. Whether you're already a reading superstar or trying to improve your skills, this chapter is packed with tips, strategies, and real-life scenarios to help you crush sixth-grade reading and maybe even discover some new favorite books along the way.

1. Think Beyond the Plot
In sixth grade, it's not enough to know what happens in a story. You'll need to dig into why things happen and what they mean. Pay attention to themes, character motivations, and the connections between events.

Real-Life Scenario:
You're reading Holes by Louis Sachar, and your teacher asks why Stanley's family feels cursed. Instead of just saying, "Because of the shoes," you dig deeper and explain how it connects to the theme of justice and breaking family cycles. Your teacher nods, impressed by your thoughtful answer.

2. Keep a Reading Journal
A reading journal helps you track your thoughts, favorite quotes, and questions about what you're reading. Writing things down makes it easier to remember important details later.

Real-Life Scenario:
You're reading Wonder by R.J. Palacio and jot down, "Why does Julian act mean to Auggie?" Later, when you get to the part about Julian's insecurity, you flip back to your question and feel like a detective solving the mystery.

3. Learn to Annotate
Annotating means writing notes in the margins of your book or on sticky notes as you read. Highlight key ideas, underline new vocabulary, and jot down questions or reactions.

Real-Life Scenario:
You're reading an article about climate change for science class. You underline "greenhouse gases" and write "How do they trap heat?" in the margin. During the class discussion, you ask your question and feel proud of how prepared you are.

4. Explore Different Genres
Sixth grade is the perfect time to step outside your comfort zone. If you usually read fantasy, try a biography. If you love action, check out a mystery. Exploring new genres helps you discover stories you never knew you'd love.

Real-Life Scenario:
You pick up Hidden Figures by Margot Lee Shetterly after your teacher recommends it. Even though it's nonfiction, the story about brilliant women solving NASA's problems is so exciting, it feels like a novel.

5. Ask Big Questions
Great readers ask questions while they read. Wondering why, how, and what if keeps your brain engaged and helps you understand the text on a deeper level.

Real-Life Scenario:
As you read Percy Jackson and the Olympians, you may wonder, "Why does Percy feel like he doesn't belong in the real world?" When you realize it's because he's part of a world that most people can't see, it makes his struggles more relatable—and the story even cooler.

6. Practice Summarizing
Being able to summarize what you've read is a key skill in sixth grade. Focus on the main idea and the most important details, but skip the extra fluff.

Real-Life Scenario:
After finishing a chapter of The Giver by Lois Lowry, you summarize: "Jonas starts seeing colors, which shows he's different from everyone else in his community." When your teacher asks for a recap in class, your answer is clear and to the point.

7. Understand the Author's Purpose
Every text has a purpose—whether it's to inform, entertain, or persuade. Figuring out the author's purpose helps you see the bigger picture of what you're reading.

Real-Life Scenario:
You're reading a persuasive article about why schools should offer healthier lunches. You recognize that the author is trying to persuade readers by using facts about nutrition and stories from students. When your teacher asks for examples of persuasion, you're ready.

8. Use Context Clues for Vocabulary

In sixth grade, you'll come across harder words. Instead of grabbing a dictionary right away, look for clues in the sentence to figure out what the word means.

Real-Life Scenario:

You read, "The protagonist's resolve was unshakable, even in the face of danger." Despite not knowing what "resolve" means, the sentence implies determination. You feel proud for cracking the meaning on your own.

9. Compare Texts

Your teacher might ask you to compare two texts or find connections between what you're reading and other subjects. Look for similarities and differences to strengthen your understanding.

Real-Life Scenario:

You're reading Number the Stars by Lois Lowry and notice how it connects to what you learned in social studies about World War II. In your essay, you write about how the book shows the bravery of ordinary people during the war.

10. Read Actively, Not Passively

Don't just let the words float past you—engage with them! Picture the scenes, imagine how the characters feel, and think about what might happen next.

Real-Life Scenario:

While reading Hatchet by Gary Paulsen, you imagine what it would be like to survive alone in the wilderness. You think about what you'd do differently from Brian, which helps you stay hooked on the story.

11. Share Your Thoughts

Talking about books with classmates or friends makes reading more fun. Share your favorite parts, discuss themes, or debate about characters' decisions.

Real-Life Scenario:

During a class discussion on The Lightning Thief, you say, "I think Annabeth is a wonderful character because she's smart and brave." A classmate adds, "But sometimes she can be a little bossy." You realize both viewpoints make sense, and the discussion makes the book even more interesting.

12. Use Reading Goals to Challenge Yourself

Set goals to push yourself as a reader. Maybe you want to finish a certain number of books, tackle a harder novel, or read more nonfiction this semester.

Real-Life Scenario:

You challenge yourself to read The Hobbit by J.R.R. Tolkien, even though it's longer and has tricky language. It takes time, but when you finish, you feel like you've conquered a mountain.

13. Reflect on What You've Read

After finishing a book, take a moment to think about what you learned and how it made you feel. Reflecting helps you remember the story and connect with it more deeply.

Real-Life Scenario:

After finishing A Wrinkle in Time, you realize how much you admired Meg's bravery and growth. You write in your reading journal, "Meg's story showed me that it's okay to be scared as long as you keep trying."

Final Thought

Reading in sixth grade is about more than just flipping pages—it's about diving into new worlds, asking big questions, and thinking deeply about what you discover. For fun or class, these strategies will help you succeed and make reading a highlight of your day. So grab a book, settle into a cozy spot, and let the adventure begin. You've got this, sixth-grade reader!

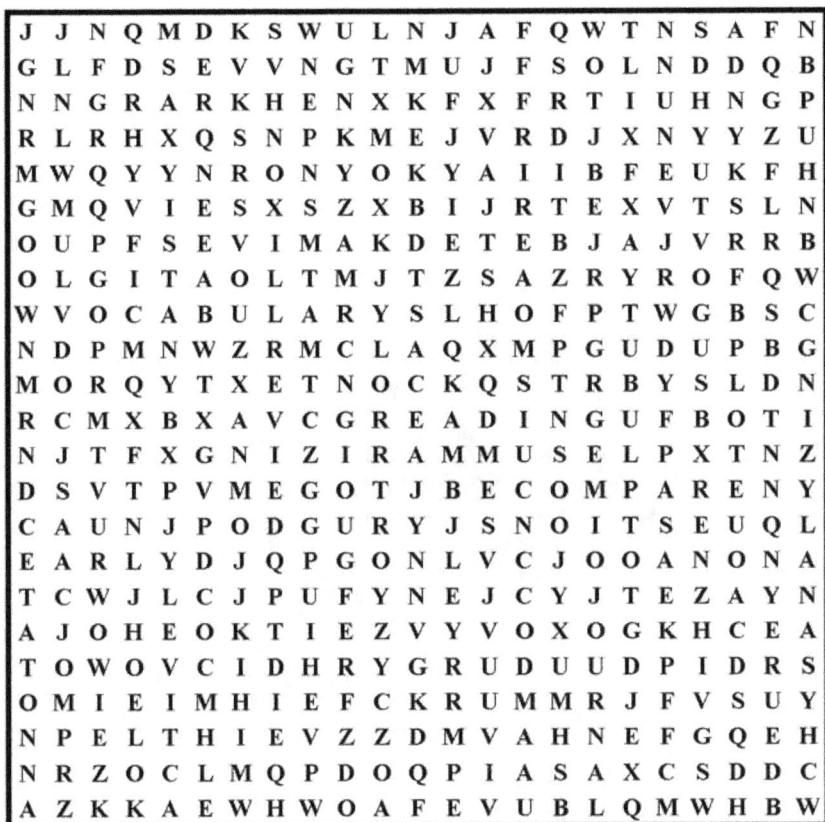

actively	genres	questions
analyzing	goals	reading
annotate	journal	summarizing
compare	plot	texts
context	purpose	vocabulary

Chapter 10

How to Succeed in Physical Education in Sixth Grade

Hey there, sixth-grade athlete! Physical education (P.E.) in sixth grade isn't just about running laps or playing games—it's about challenging yourself, learning teamwork, and building skills that will help you stay active and healthy. This year, you'll probably face new sports, tougher fitness tests, and more complex strategies. But don't worry—with the right attitude and a little preparation, you'll crush it in P.E. and maybe even have some fun along the way. Ready to step up your game? Let's dive into some tips, strategies, and real-life sixth-grade scenarios to help you succeed in P.E..

1. Be Ready to Try New Things
Sixth grade P.E. often includes sports and activities you've never tried before, like volleyball, track and field, or even yoga. It's okay if you're not great at something right away—what matters is that you give it a try.

Real-Life Scenario:
Your P.E. teacher introduces badminton, and you've never played before. At first, you miss the shuttlecock every time you swing, but after a few tries, you get the hang of it. By the end of class, you're having fun and scoring points with your partner.

2. Dress for Success
The right gear can make a huge difference in how comfortable and confident you feel during P.E. Wear sneakers with good grip, clothes you can move in, and bring a water bottle to stay hydrated.

Real-Life Scenario:
You forget your sneakers one day and have to run in flats. Your feet hurt, and you can't keep up during sprints. The next day, you double-check your P.E. bag and feel much more prepared.

3. Warm Up Like a Pro
Warming up before activities helps prevent injuries and gets your body ready to perform. Take warm-ups seriously—don't just go through the motions.

Real-Life Scenario:
Before a soccer game, your class does stretches and jogs around the field. You notice that when you warm up properly, you feel faster and less tired during the game. Plus, you don't pull a muscle like your friend who skipped warm-ups.

4. Learn the Rules of the Game
Knowing the rules of a sport helps you play better and avoids arguments with teammates or opponents. Pay attention when your teacher explains how to play, and don't be afraid to ask questions.

Real-Life Scenario:
Your P.E. class starts a flag football unit, and you're not sure what "offside" means. You ask your teacher, and they explain it with a quick example. Now you understand the rule, and your team avoids penalties.

5. Practice Good Sportsmanship

Winning feels great, but how you treat others during and after the game matters even more. Cheer for your teammates, congratulate the other team, and don't let losing ruin your day.

Real-Life Scenario:

Your team loses a close basketball game, and you feel disappointed. Instead of sulking, you high-five the winning team and tell them, "Great job!" They respect your positive attitude, and you leave the game feeling proud of your effort.

6. Push Yourself During Fitness Tests

Fitness tests like the pacer, push-ups, and sit-ups might seem intimidating, but they're a chance to see how much you've improved. Set personal goals and focus on doing your best, not just beating others.

Real-Life Scenario:

Last year, you could only do 10 push-ups. For this year's test, you practice at home and set a goal to reach 15. When the test comes, you hit 17 and feel like a rockstar.

7. Be a Team Player

P.E. isn't just about individual skills—it's about working with others. Pass the ball, share ideas, and encourage your teammates to do their best.

Real-Life Scenario:

During a volleyball game, one of your teammates keeps missing the ball. Instead of getting frustrated, you say, "You've got this! Try again!" Your encouragement helps them improve, and your team works better together.

8. Learn to Handle Constructive Criticism

In sixth grade, your teacher might give you specific tips to improve your technique. Instead of taking it personally, see it as a chance to get better.

Real-Life Scenario:

Your P.E. teacher tells you to keep your knees bent when shooting a basketball. You try it during practice and notice your shots are more accurate. Listening to advice pays off!

9. Stay Positive During Challenges

Not every activity will be easy, and that's okay. Keep a positive attitude, even if you're struggling with a new skill or sport.

Real-Life Scenario:

Your class starts a gymnastics unit, and you're terrible at cartwheels. Instead of giving up, you keep practicing and laugh at your wobbly attempts. By the end of the unit, you can do a decent cartwheel—and you've had fun along the way.

10. Use Strategy, Not Just Speed

In sixth grade, P.E. often includes more strategy-based games, like capture the flag or ultimate frisbee. Think about your moves and work with your teammates to outsmart the other team.

Real-Life Scenario:

During a capture-the-flag game, you notice the other team always leaves one side unguarded. You tell your team, and together you sneak in and grab the flag. Your strategic thinking helps your team win!

11. Respect Everyone's Abilities

Not everyone in your class will be a star athlete, and that's okay. Encourage your classmates, no matter their skill level, and focus on making P.E. fun for everyone.

Real-Life Scenario:
A classmate is nervous about trying out for relay races. You say, "You've got this—just run your best!" They smile, give it their all, and thank you for being supportive.

12. Celebrate Small Wins

Improvement takes time, so celebrate your progress, even if it's small. Whether you're running faster, scoring more points, or just having fun, every win matters.

Real-Life Scenario:
You finally hit a tennis ball over the net after weeks of missing. Your teacher cheers, and you feel proud of how far you've come.

Final Thought

P.E. in sixth grade is your chance to stay active, learn new skills, and grow as a team player. By staying positive, encouraging others, and giving your best effort, you'll succeed in ways that go beyond just winning games. So lace up those sneakers, grab that ball, and show your P.E. class what you're made of. You've got this, sixth-grade athlete!

Chapter 10 How to Succeed in Physical Education in Sixth Grade

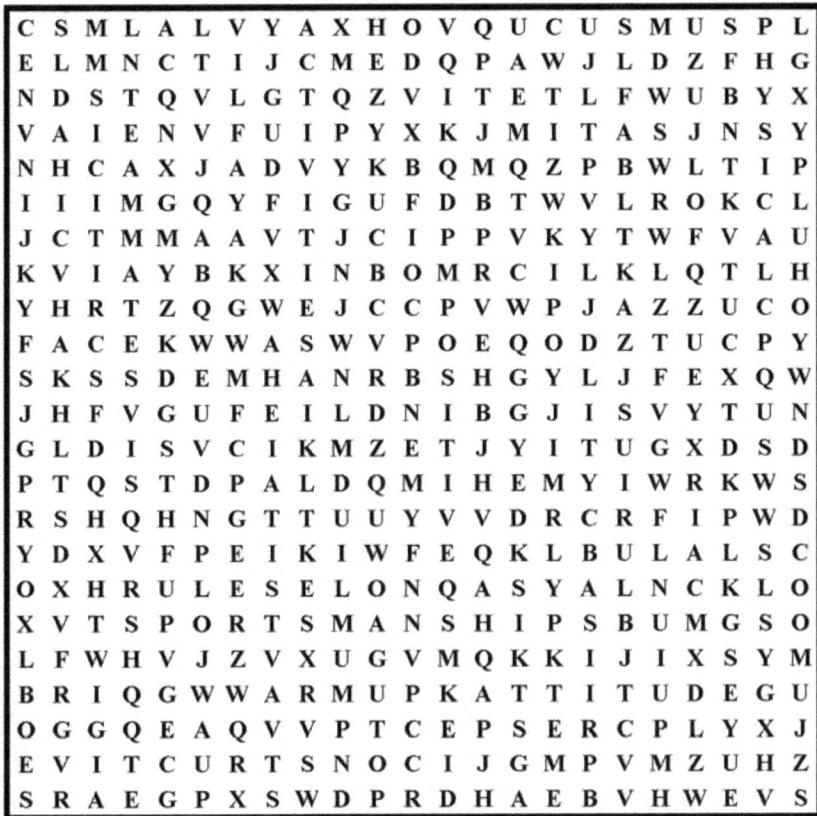

C	S	M	L	A	L	V	Y	A	X	H	O	V	Q	U	C	U	S	M	U	S	P	L
E	L	M	N	C	T	I	J	C	M	E	D	Q	P	A	W	J	L	D	Z	F	H	G
N	D	S	T	Q	V	L	G	T	Q	Z	V	I	T	E	T	L	F	W	U	B	Y	X
V	A	I	E	N	V	F	U	I	P	Y	X	K	J	M	I	T	A	S	J	N	S	Y
N	H	C	A	X	J	A	D	V	Y	K	B	Q	M	Q	Z	P	B	W	L	T	I	P
I	I	I	M	G	Q	Y	F	I	G	U	F	D	B	T	W	V	L	R	O	K	C	L
J	C	T	M	M	A	A	V	T	J	C	I	P	P	V	K	Y	T	W	F	V	A	U
K	V	I	A	Y	B	K	X	I	N	B	O	M	R	C	I	L	K	L	Q	T	L	H
Y	H	R	T	Z	Q	G	W	E	J	C	C	P	V	W	P	J	A	Z	Z	U	C	O
F	A	C	E	K	W	W	A	S	W	V	P	O	E	Q	O	D	Z	T	U	C	P	Y
S	K	S	S	D	E	M	H	A	N	R	B	S	H	G	Y	L	J	F	E	X	Q	W
J	H	F	V	G	U	F	E	I	L	D	N	I	B	G	J	I	S	V	Y	T	U	N
G	L	D	I	S	V	C	I	K	M	Z	E	T	J	Y	I	T	U	G	X	D	S	D
P	T	Q	S	T	D	P	A	L	D	Q	M	I	H	E	M	Y	I	W	R	K	W	S
R	S	H	Q	H	N	G	T	T	U	U	Y	V	V	D	R	C	R	F	I	P	W	D
Y	D	X	V	F	P	E	I	K	I	W	F	E	Q	K	L	B	U	L	A	L	S	C
O	X	H	R	U	L	E	S	E	L	O	N	Q	A	S	Y	A	L	N	C	K	L	O
X	V	T	S	P	O	R	T	S	M	A	N	S	H	I	P	S	B	U	M	G	S	O
L	F	W	H	V	J	Z	V	X	U	G	V	M	Q	K	K	I	J	I	X	S	Y	M
B	R	I	Q	G	W	W	A	R	M	U	P	K	A	T	T	I	T	U	D	E	G	U
O	G	G	Q	E	A	Q	V	V	P	T	C	E	P	S	E	R	C	P	L	Y	X	J
E	V	I	T	C	U	R	T	S	N	O	C	I	J	G	M	P	V	M	Z	U	H	Z
S	R	A	E	G	P	X	S	W	D	P	R	D	H	A	E	B	V	H	W	E	V	S

activities	fitness	rules
attitude	gear	skills
constructive	physical	sportsmanship
criticism	positive	teammates
education	respect	warmup

Chapter 11

How to Succeed in Science in Sixth Grade

Hey there, sixth-grade scientist! Science in sixth grade isn't just about learning facts—it's about becoming a detective of the natural world. You'll be conducting experiments, analyzing data, and discovering how the universe works. This year, you'll explore topics like energy, ecosystems, weather patterns, and even the mysteries of space. But how can you succeed when the material gets more challenging? Don't worry! This chapter is packed with tips, strategies, and real-life sixth-grade scenarios to help you shine in science class.

1. Get Curious About Everything

Science is all about curiosity. Ask questions about the world around you and use your lessons to find answers. The more curious you are, the more exciting science will feel.

Real-Life Scenario:

Your teacher explains how earthquakes happen because of tectonic plates shifting. You wonder, "Does this occur where I live?" You look it up and learn your area has a small fault line. Now, you can't wait to learn more about Earth's layers in class.

2. Be Ready to Experiment

In sixth grade, you'll do more hands-on experiments. This is your chance to test ideas and see science in action. Follow the steps carefully and don't be afraid to make mistakes—that's how real scientists learn.

Real-Life Scenario:

Your group is testing which type of paper towel absorbs the most water. You think the thickest will win, but the thinner brand absorbs more. Instead of being upset, you're excited to share your unexpected results with the class.

3. Take Detailed Notes
Science involves lots of facts, formulas, and observations. Writing detailed notes during lessons and labs will help you remember important information when it's time to study or write a report.

Real-Life Scenario:
During a lab on chemical reactions, you write down every step, including how the vinegar fizzed when it hit the baking soda. Later, when your teacher asks you to explain what happened, your notes help you recall the reaction perfectly.

4. Use Visual Aids
Diagrams, charts, and graphs are super important in science. They help you understand complex ideas and make your notes more fun and easier to review.

Real-Life Scenario:
You're studying the water cycle. Instead of just reading about evaporation and precipitation, you draw a colorful diagram with arrows showing how water moves through the system. When it's time for a quiz, your visual memory helps you nail it.

5. Master Scientific Vocabulary
Science has its own language—words like photosynthesis, atom, and ecosystem. Understanding these terms makes it easier to follow lessons and answer questions.

Real-Life Scenario:
Your teacher says, "Today we'll learn about producers, consumers, and decomposers." You write a quick definition of each:

- Producers make energy from the sun.
- Consumers eat other organisms.
- Decomposers break down dead material.

When you're asked to identify each in an ecosystem, you feel confident.

6. Ask Thoughtful Questions
When something doesn't make sense, don't hesitate to ask. Thoughtful questions help you understand the material and show your teacher you're engaged.

Real-Life Scenario:
During a lesson on weather, your teacher explains how warm air rises. You ask, "How does that create a thunderstorm?" Your teacher uses your question to explain the whole process, and your classmates thank you for speaking up.

7. Learn to Analyze Data
In sixth grade, you'll work with data like charts, graphs, and tables. Practice looking for patterns and figuring out what the data is telling you.

Real-Life Scenario:
Your class measures the temperature of water at different depths in a lake. You notice the surface is warmer than the bottom and realize sunlight warms the top layers. Sharing this observation impresses your teacher and your group.

8. Stay Organized During Labs

Science labs have lots of steps and materials. Keep everything organized, label your data clearly, and double-check your work to avoid mistakes.

Real-Life Scenario:
During a chemistry experiment, your group mixes two substances in the wrong order because you didn't check the instructions. The reaction doesn't work, but you learn the importance of following the procedure carefully.

9. Use Technology to Explore

From simulations to videos, technology can bring science to life. Use online tools to explore concepts you don't fully understand in class.

Real-Life Scenario:
You're learning about space and find a website with a virtual tour of the solar system. Exploring planets up close helps you understand their size and distance better, and you can't wait to share your discoveries in class.

10. Work Well with Your Lab Partners

In sixth grade, you'll often work in teams. Listen to everyone's ideas, divide tasks fairly, and stay focused on the experiment.

Real-Life Scenario:
Your group is building a paper bridge to test weight limits. You suggest folding the paper for strength, while another teammate adds support beams. By combining ideas, your bridge holds more weight than anyone else's.

11. Study Like a Scientist

When studying for a science test, focus on understanding concepts, not just memorizing facts. Use practice questions, flashcards, or even create your own mini-experiments to reinforce your learning.

Real-Life Scenario:

Before a test on energy, you create a flashcard for each type: kinetic, potential, thermal, and chemical. Quizzing yourself helps you remember the differences, and you feel ready to ace the exam.

12. Embrace Mistakes

Science is all about learning from failure. If an experiment doesn't work or you get an answer wrong, use it as an opportunity to figure out why.

Real-Life Scenario:

Your solar-powered car moves slowly during a class competition. Instead of feeling disappointed, you adjust the angle of the solar panel and try again. The car speeds up, and you feel proud of your problem-solving skills.

13. Think About the "So What?"

In sixth grade, it's important to think about why what you're learning matters. How does it connect to the real world or your own life?

Real-Life Scenario:

In an ecosystems unit, you discover how deforestation impacts animal habitats. You realize this is why recycling and planting trees are important—and you decide to join an environmental club.

Final Thought

Sixth grade science is all about thinking like a scientist—asking questions, testing ideas, and exploring how the world works. By staying curious, organized, and ready to learn from mistakes, you'll not only succeed in class but also discover how amazing science can be. So grab your goggles, dive into those experiments, and show your class what a true sixth-grade scientist looks like. You've got this!

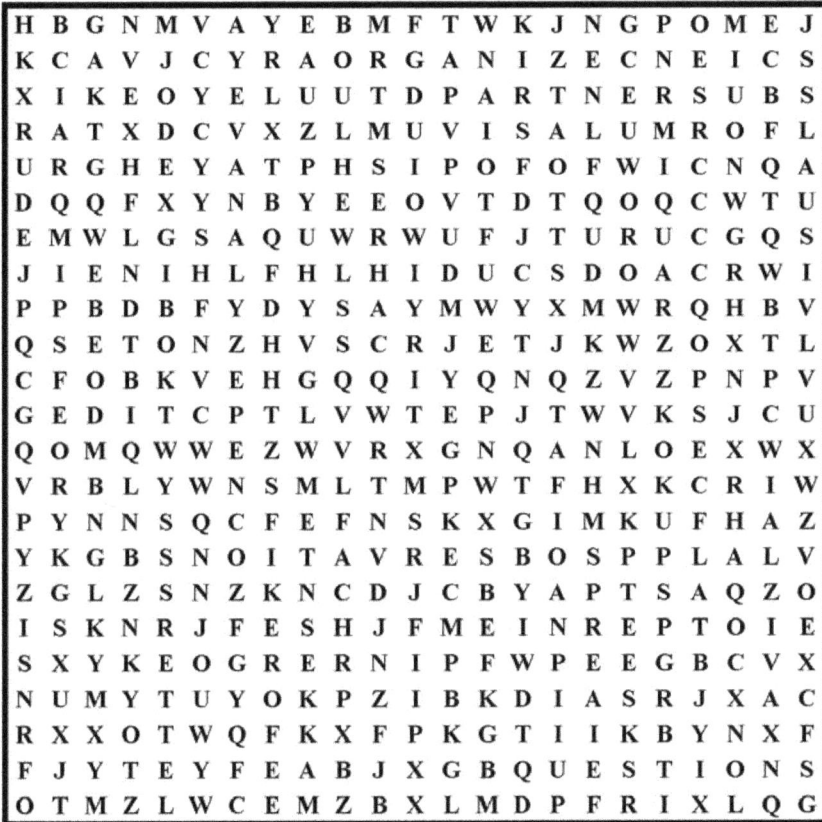

H B G N M V A Y E B M F T W K J N G P O M E J
K C A V J C Y R A O R G A N I Z E C N E I C S
X I K E O Y E L U U T D P A R T N E R S U B S
R A T X D C V X Z L M U V I S A L U M R O F L
U R G H E Y A T P H S I P O F O F W I C N Q A
D Q Q F X Y N B Y E E O V T D T Q O Q C W T U
E M W L G S A Q U W R W U F J T U R U C G Q S
J I E N I H L F H L H I D U C S D O A C R W I
P P B D B F Y D Y S A Y M W Y X M W R Q H B V
Q S E T O N Z H V S C R J E T J K W Z O X T L
C F O B K V E H G Q Q I Y Q N Q Z V Z P N P V
G E D I T C P T L V W T E P J T W V K S J C U
Q O M Q W W E Z W V R X G N Q A N L O E X W X
V R B L Y W N S M L T M P W T F H X K C R I W
P Y N N S Q C F E F N S K X G I M K U F H A Z
Y K G B S N O I T A V R E S B O S P P L A L V
Z G L Z S N Z K N C D J C B Y A P T S A Q Z O
I S K N R J F E S H J F M E I N R E P T O I E
S X Y K E O G R E R N I P F W P E E G B C V X
N U M Y T U Y O K P Z I B K D I A S R J X A C
R X X O T W Q F K X F P K G T I I K B Y N X F
F J Y T E Y F E A B J X G B Q U E S T I O N S
O T M Z L W C E M Z B X L M D P F R I X L Q G

analyze	lab	questions
curious	notes	science
experiment	observations	scientist
facts	organize	visuals
formulas	partners	vocabulary

Chapter 12

How to Write Successfully in Sixth Grade

Hey there, sixth-grade writer! Writing in sixth grade is a whole new adventure. This year, you'll tackle essays, stories, research projects, and even some creative writing that will push your skills to the next level. Writing isn't just about spelling words right or having neat handwriting—it's about expressing your thoughts clearly, convincing others, and maybe even telling stories that blow people's minds. Whether you love writing or are just hoping to survive it, this chapter is packed with tips, tricks, and real-life scenarios to help you succeed. Ready to become a sixth-grade writing champ? Let's dive in!

1. Start with a Strong Plan

Before you start writing, take time to brainstorm and organize your ideas. Sixth grade writing is about structure, so planning ahead is like building a solid foundation for a house.

Real-Life Scenario:

You're assigned a persuasive essay about whether kids should have more recess. Instead of jumping straight into writing, you jot down ideas like:

- More time to burn energy = better focus
- Exercise is good for health
- Extra recess builds social skills

With your main points in place, your essay practically writes itself.

2. Write an Attention-Grabbing Introduction

Your introduction is your chance to hook your reader. Start with a surprising fact, a question, or a bold statement that makes them want to keep reading.

Real-Life Scenario:
Instead of starting your report on climate change with, "Climate change is a problem," try: "Every year, glaciers shrink by 267 billion tons of ice—enough to fill over 100 million Olympic swimming pools. What's causing this? Let's dive in." Your teacher will be impressed, and you'll feel like a pro.

3. Show, Don't Tell
In sixth grade, good writing means painting a picture with your words. Use sensory details and examples to make your writing come alive.

Real-Life Scenario:
Instead of writing, "The dog was excited," you write, "The dog's tail wagged so hard it thumped against the wall, and it jumped up and down, barking like it couldn't contain itself." Your reader can see and feel the excitement.

4. Use Strong Paragraphs
Every paragraph should have one main idea, and it should start with a clear topic sentence. Support it with examples, facts, or details, and end with a sentence that ties everything together.

Real-Life Scenario:
You're writing about why students should read more books. Your paragraph might look like this:

- **Topic sentence:** "Reading improves your imagination."
- **Supporting detail:** "Books take you to magical worlds, like Hogwarts or Narnia, where anything is possible."
- **Wrap-up:** "By diving into stories, you train your brain to think creatively."

5. Transition Smoothly Between Ideas

Good writing flows like a river. Use transition words like however, for example, or as a result to guide your reader from one idea to the next.

Real-Life Scenario:

In a report on space exploration, instead of jumping from one point to another, you write: "While landing on the Moon was a huge milestone, recent missions to Mars are taking space exploration even further." Smooth transitions make your writing feel professional.

6. Edit Like a Detective

Great writing doesn't happen in the first draft. The real magic occurs during the editing process. Look for spelling mistakes, awkward sentences, or places where you can add more detail.

Real-Life Scenario:

You finish a short story but notice one sentence feels off: "The sky was dark, and the storm was loud." You revise it to, "Thunder rumbled through the pitch-black sky as lightning cracked across the horizon." Boom! Now your story packs a punch.

7. Use a Variety of Sentences

Mixing up short and long sentences keeps your writing interesting. Too many short sentences can feel choppy, while too many long ones can feel overwhelming.

Real-Life Scenario:

In an essay about your favorite holiday, instead of: "We eat dinner. We open presents. Then we play games."
Try:
"We eat a big, delicious dinner together. Afterward, we tear into the presents under the tree. By the time we're done, the living room looks like a wrapping-paper explosion!"

8. Back Up Your Opinions

When writing persuasive essays or arguments, support your points with evidence. Use facts, examples, or quotes to make your case convincing.

Real-Life Scenario:

You're arguing for longer lunches. Instead of just saying, "Lunch is too short," you write, "Studies show that students with longer lunches are more focused and perform better in the afternoon." Your teacher is impressed by your use of research.

9. Practice Writing Across Genres

Sixth grade is the perfect time to try different types of writing, from narratives and poetry to informative essays and research reports. Each genre helps you grow as a writer.

Real-Life Scenario:

Your teacher assigns a science fiction story, and you've never written one before. You imagine what the world might look like in 100 years and create a story about a girl exploring Mars. Trying something new makes writing exciting.

10. Keep Your Reader in Mind

Think about who will be reading your work. Is it your teacher? Your classmates? A contest judge? Write in a way that grabs their attention and matches the tone they expect.

Real-Life Scenario:

For a class presentation, you keep your tone professional: "The American Revolution was a turning point in history." But for a funny creative story, you let your personality shine: "If I had a pet dragon, we'd never lose a game of dodgeball."

11. Ask for Feedback

Sharing your work with others can help you improve. A teacher, friend, or family member can catch mistakes you missed or give ideas to make your writing stronger.

Real-Life Scenario:

You write a poem about summer but feel like it's missing something. You show it to your best friend, who suggests adding more sensory details like the smell of sunscreen or the sound of waves. Their advice makes your poem even better.

12. Celebrate Your Growth

Writing can be hard, but every word you write makes you better. Celebrate the small wins, like finishing a tough assignment or getting positive feedback.

Real-Life Scenario:

You struggle with your first research report but keep practicing. By the end of the semester, you turn in a polished essay on endangered species, and your teacher writes, "Great improvement!" on your paper. You feel proud of how far you've come.

Final Thought

Writing in sixth grade is about finding your voice, exploring new ideas, and learning how to share your thoughts in powerful ways. Whether you're crafting a story, persuading your teacher in an essay, or reporting on a science project, these tips will help you succeed. So grab a notebook, let your imagination run wild, and show the world what an amazing writer you are. You've got this, sixth-grade author!

```
K Z F W N I I B Y F S E C N E T N E S E W K V
K W J R Q P F J U X E U Y S N O I N I P O Q W
Z R B M L J C E Q D P E Z K L Y L S W E Y A B
T E W A R V D V G N W B D E H C L Y T R S J K
Q R N R E W L I G N R J A B S R S A H S L C A
C B P P H O Z D S Y I W O H A W L S W U W G F
H L W T W B Q E F Z T L A R T C T S B A M C V
D O Z J C T W N A K I P J E J O K E R S G D X
E P H E W O S C W W N D E T A I L S A I O G K
D L O B H P C E Z F G D L F K F V N I V R N N
U D G S Z W I N T R O D U C T I O N N E V T O
O M F A H U P W V Y V L C P O M D I S H C Y Q
R A B U S G O O T Y W Z W A H T I P T Q F P J
Z J Z R H Q T Z R F N X U S P A X A O R M P G
R Z T A P L L S H R Y S E Y U O F R R G C R N
W T P O A C D X L X O H J I L U V Q M Y R W N
Y D M M R L G D L U H O J M P V M G R Z V B J
R H B S G V K X O A P D J C Z A D E M Z X T X
H A O T A I O W Y W Z Y L G O D E L U H W P A
U R X X R P S X S R G Y G W M Q D G G N I S W
Z U E F A N S L N O X I Y S K H I B P U C R X
E V X V P T U S E G F X L W M Y T L G Y V R E
N J Y I J T D Z I S Q Z Y N I G Z H A U D L S
```

brainstorm	feedback	plan
details	introduction	sentences
edit	opinions	show
essays	paragraphs	topic
evidence	persuasive	writing

Chapter 13

How to Master Homework in Sixth Grade

1. Make Homework Part of Your Routine
In sixth grade, you've got more responsibilities, so having a homework routine is a game-changer. Decide when and where you'll do your homework every day and stick to it.

Real-Life Scenario:
You decide to tackle homework right after dinner at the kitchen table. Every night at 6:30 PM, you pull out your assignments. After a week, it feels natural, and you stop dreading it because you know it's just part of your evening.

2. Create a Homework Survival Kit
Keep everything you need—pencils, erasers, highlighters, a calculator, and notebooks—ready to go in one spot. No more wasting time searching for supplies!

Real-Life Scenario:
One day, your science project instructions say you need colored pencils. Without searching, you grab them from your homework survival kit and start working. Boom—no time wasted!

3. Start with the Tough Stuff
It's wise to start with the most challenging assignments as your mind is at its peak. Once the tough stuff is out of the way, the rest feels easier.

Real-Life Scenario:
You have a math worksheet, a social studies reading, and a vocabulary list that need to be studied. You know math takes the most brainpower, so you do it first. After that, reading about ancient Egypt and reviewing words becomes effortless.

4. Break It Down into Chunks
Big assignments can feel intimidating, so break them into smaller, manageable pieces. Take it one step at a time.

Real-Life Scenario:
Your teacher assigns a five-paragraph essay due next week. Rather than waiting until the last minute, you plan ahead:

- **Monday:** Brainstorm ideas.
- **Tuesday:** Write the introduction.
- **Wednesday:** Write two body paragraphs.
- **Thursday:** Write the rest and edit.
- **By Friday,** your essay is ready, and you're stress-free.

5. Use a Planner (Seriously, It Helps!)
Write down your homework in a planner or an app. This way, you'll never forget assignments or miss due dates.

Real-Life Scenario:
Your math teacher assigns a project due next Friday, and your English teacher gives a book report due next Monday. You jot both down in your planner and set reminders to work on them throughout the week. You finish both on time and avoid last-minute panic.

6. Eliminate Distractions

It's hard to focus when your phone is buzzing, or the TV is on. Create a quiet, distraction-free zone for homework time.

Real-Life Scenario:

You're halfway through a reading assignment when your phone buzzes with a text. You pick it up, and suddenly 20 minutes are gone. The next day, you put your phone in another room during homework. You finish faster and have more time to chill afterward.

7. Ask for Help When You're Stuck

Don't waste hours stuck on one problem. If you're confused, ask a parent, teacher, or friend for help. It's better to get clarification than guess.

Real-Life Scenario:

You're struggling with a long-division problem in math. Instead of staring at it for 30 minutes, you ask your older sibling to explain it. They show you a shortcut, and suddenly it all makes sense.

8. Use Online Resources

When you need extra help, check out educational videos, websites, or apps. Just make sure you're using trusted sources.

Real-Life Scenario:

Your science homework asks you to explain how a food web works, but you don't quite understand. You watch a quick video online that explains it with examples, and suddenly you're ready to write a detailed answer.

9. Take Short Breaks

Working for hours without a break can burn you out. Use the "25-5 rule": work for 25 minutes, then break for 5 minutes to get a snack, stretch, or relax.

Real-Life Scenario:

You're working on a history worksheet and start feeling tired. You set a timer for a quick break, get some water, and come back feeling refreshed and ready to finish.

10. Double-Check Before You're Done

Before calling it a night, go over your work to catch mistakes or incomplete answers. A quick review can make a big difference.

Real-Life Scenario:

You're about to hand in your math homework when you notice you skipped problem #7. You quickly solve it, saving yourself from losing points.

11. Reward Yourself

Give yourself something to look forward to after finishing your homework. Rewards can be small, like watching your favorite show or having a treat.

Real-Life Scenario:

You tell yourself, "Once I finish my spelling sentences, I can play 20 minutes of my favorite video game." You power through your homework and enjoy guilt-free gaming time.

12. Learn from Feedback

When teachers return graded homework, take a close look at their comments. Use their feedback to improve next time.

Real-Life Scenario:

Your teacher marks a question wrong on your science homework because you mixed up "mitosis" and "meiosis." You write a note in your science notebook to review the difference before the next test.

13. Don't Overload Yourself

If you're feeling overwhelmed with homework and activities, talk to your teacher or parents. They can help you find ways to manage your workload.

Real-Life Scenario:

You're juggling soccer practice, a school play rehearsal, and three homework assignments. You tell your teacher you're struggling to keep up, and they extend the due date for one assignment. Now you can focus and get everything done without stressing.

14. Celebrate Your Wins

Finished all your homework on time? Pat yourself on the back. Recognizing your achievements helps build confidence and keeps you motivated.

Real-Life Scenario:

You complete a challenging book report early, and your teacher gives you a shoutout in class. You feel proud and realize that planning ahead really works.

Final Thought

Mastering homework in sixth grade isn't about being perfect—it's about being consistent, organized, and willing to ask for help when you need it. With these tips, you'll stay ahead of your assignments, impress your teachers, and still have time to enjoy life outside of school. So grab your planner, sharpen your pencils, and show sixth grade homework who's boss. You've got this!

Chapter 13 How to Master Homework in Sixth Grade

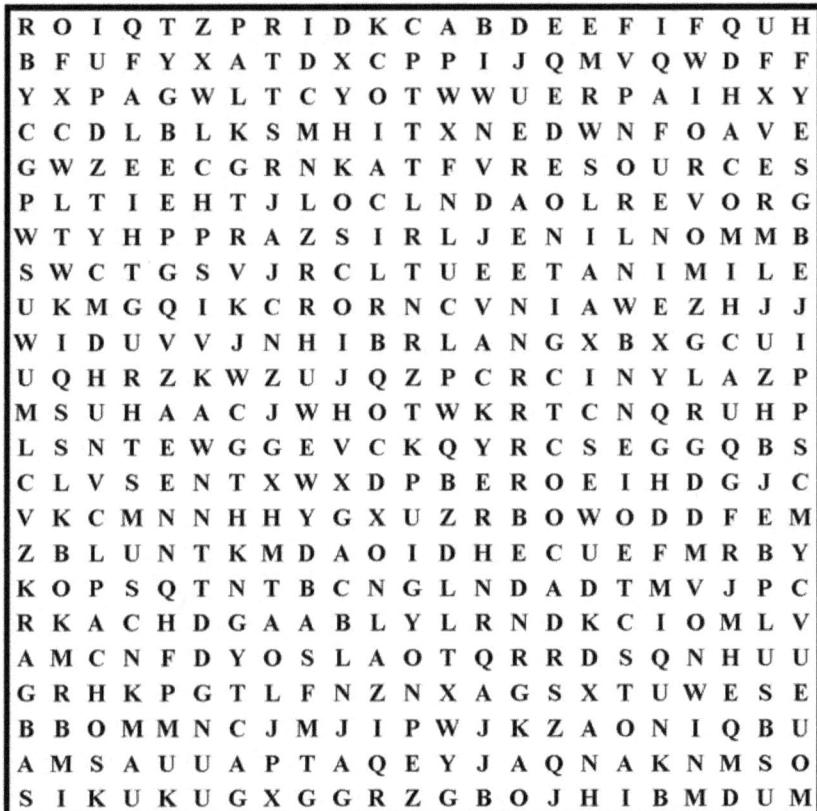

```
R O I Q T Z P R I D K C A B D E E F I F Q U H
B F U F Y X A T D X C P P I J Q M V Q W D F F
Y X P A G W L T C Y O T W W U E R P A I H X Y
C C D L B L K S M H I T X N E D W N F O A V E
G W Z E E C G R N K A T F V R E S O U R C E S
P L T I E H T J L O C L N D A O L R E V O R G
W T Y H P P R A Z S I R L J E N I L N O M M B
S W C T G S V J R C L T U E E T A N I M I L E
U K M G Q I K C R O R N C V N I A W E Z H J J
W I D U V V J N H I B R L A N G X B X G C U I
U Q H R Z K W Z U J Q Z P C R C I N Y L A Z P
M S U H A A C J W H O T W K R T C N Q R U H P
L S N T E W G G E V C K Q Y R C S E G G Q B S
C L V S E N T X W X D P B E R O E I H D G J C
V K C M N N H H Y G X U Z R B O W O D D F E M
Z B L U N T K M D A O I D H E C U E F M R B Y
K O P S Q T N T B C N G L N D A D T M V J P C
R K A C H D G A A B L Y L R N D K C I O M L V
A M C N F D Y O S L A O T Q R R D S Q N H U U
G R H K P G T L F N Z N X A G S X T U W E S E
B B O M M N C J M J I P W J K Z A O N I Q B U
A M S A U U A P T A Q E Y J A Q N A K N M S O
S I K U K U G X G G R Z G B O J H I B M D U M
```

breaks	eliminate	overload
challenging	feedback	resources
check	help	reward
chunks	homework	routine
distractions	online	survivalkit
		(survival kit)

Chapter 14

How to Study for Exams in Sixth Grade

Hey there, sixth-grade scholar! Studying for exams in sixth grade is a big deal. This year, exams aren't just about remembering facts, they're about understanding concepts, making connections, and showing that you're ready to handle more complex ideas. It might seem overwhelming, but don't worry! With the right strategies and a solid plan, you'll be prepared, confident, and ready to rock your exams. This chapter is packed with tips, tricks, and real-life sixth-grade scenarios to help you succeed. Let's get started!

1. Start Studying Early
Cramming the night before doesn't work when exams cover lots of material. Start reviewing at least a week before your test so you have plenty of time to go over everything.

Real-Life Scenario:
Your science exam is next Friday, and it covers ecosystems, the water cycle, and food webs. Instead of waiting until Thursday night, you spend 20 minutes each day reviewing one topic. By Friday, you feel calm and ready to ace it.

2. Use a Study Schedule
Break your study sessions into manageable chunks and focus on one subject at a time. A schedule keeps you organized and prevents last-minute panic.

Real-Life Scenario:
You write a study plan for the week:

- **Monday:** Review social studies notes
- **Tuesday:** Practice math problems
- **Wednesday:** Quiz yourself on vocabulary
- **Thursday:** Go over everything once more

Following this plan helps you stay on track and avoid feeling overwhelmed.

3. Organize Your Materials

Before you start studying, gather everything you need—notes, textbooks, handouts, and any study guides your teacher gave you. Keeping your materials organized saves time and keeps you focused.

Real-Life Scenario:

You're preparing for a history test and realize your notes are messy. You rewrite them neatly, adding important dates and events in bold. When you study, the clean layout makes it easier to remember everything.

4. Find Your Perfect Study Spot

Select a peaceful, comfortable location free from distractions. Avoid studying in front of the TV or in a busy room.

Real-Life Scenario:

You usually do homework at the kitchen table, but your siblings keep interrupting. For exam prep, you move to your room, close the door, and turn off your phone. You focus better and finish faster.

5. Use Active Study Techniques

Active studying means engaging with the material, not just reading it. Use flashcards, practice questions, or create your own quizzes to test yourself. Flashcards are a fun and easy way to practice facts and vocabulary.

- **Supplies Needed: Index cards (any size of your choice)**
- Write a question or term on one side of an index card and the answer on the flip side.
- After creating the flashcard, read the question and then the answer.
- Read both sides of the card without trying to memorize the answer.
- Repeat the above step over and over
- Do this repeatedly each day. Soon you'll realize that you know the information without really trying to memorize it.
- Test yourself or ask a friend or family member to quiz you.
- **This works!**

Real-Life Scenario:
You're studying for a vocabulary test. Instead of rereading the list, you write each word on a flashcard with its definition on the back. You quiz yourself and feel confident when you get most of them right.

6. Teach Someone Else

Explaining something to someone else helps you remember it. Teaching forces you to organize your thoughts and figure out what you know—and what you don't.

Real-Life Scenario:
You ask your little brother to sit while you explain fractions for your math test. When he says, "I don't get it," you realize you need to review how to simplify fractions. Teaching him helps you prepare, too.

7. Take Breaks to Recharge

Your brain needs rest to process what you've studied. Use the 25-5 rule: study for 25 minutes, then take a 5-minute break to stretch, grab a snack, or relax.

Real-Life Scenario:

You're reviewing your science notes but start feeling tired after 20 minutes. You take a short break to walk around, then come back refreshed and ready to focus again.

8. Use Mnemonics and Memory Tricks

Mnemonics are phrases or tricks that help you remember information. They're especially helpful for lists, orders, or tricky facts.

Real-Life Scenario:

To remember the order of the planets, try this phrase: "My Very Eager Mom Just Saved Us Nachos" (Mercury, Venus, Earth, Mars, Jupiter, Saturn, Uranus, Neptune). It sticks in your head during the test!

9. Review Old Tests and Homework

Your teacher often uses similar questions or topics from past assignments on exams. Reviewing old tests and homework helps you see what to focus on.

Real-Life Scenario:

Before your English test, you look at an old quiz on figurative language. You notice that similes and metaphors tripped you up before, so you spend extra time reviewing those. On the test, you nail every question.

10. Study with a Friend (If It Helps)
Studying with a friend can make exam prep more fun and less stressful. Just make sure you stay on task and actually study.

Real-Life Scenario:
You and a classmate meet up to quiz each other about history facts. They ask, "What year did the Civil War start?" When you get it wrong, they help you remember it was 1861. By the end, you both feel more prepared.

11. Visualize What You're Studying
For topics like geography, science, or history, creating or looking at visuals can help. Maps, diagrams, and charts make it easier to understand complex ideas.

Real-Life Scenario:
You're studying the water cycle for science. Drawing a diagram with arrows for evaporation, condensation, and precipitation helps you remember the process during the test.

12. Stay Calm on Test Day
The morning of the exam, eat a good breakfast, take a deep breath, and remind yourself that you've prepared. Confidence is key.

Real-Life Scenario:
You walk into your math exam and see the first problem looks tricky. Instead of panicking, you skip it and move on to the ones you know. By the end, you circle back to the hard problem and realize it's not so bad after all.

13. Learn from Mistakes

If you don't do as well as you hoped, don't get discouraged. Look at what went wrong and use it to do better next time.

Real-Life Scenario:

You missed a few questions on your science test because you skipped studying the water cycle. Next time, you write out a list of all the topics in the study guide and make sure to cover each one.

Final Thought

Studying for exams in sixth grade is more than just memorizing—it's about building skills that will help you for years to come. By starting early, staying organized, and using these tips, you'll walk into your exams feeling prepared and confident. So grab your notes, sharpen your pencils, and show your exams who's boss. You've got this, sixth-grade scholar!

Chapter 14 How to Study for Exams in Sixth Grade

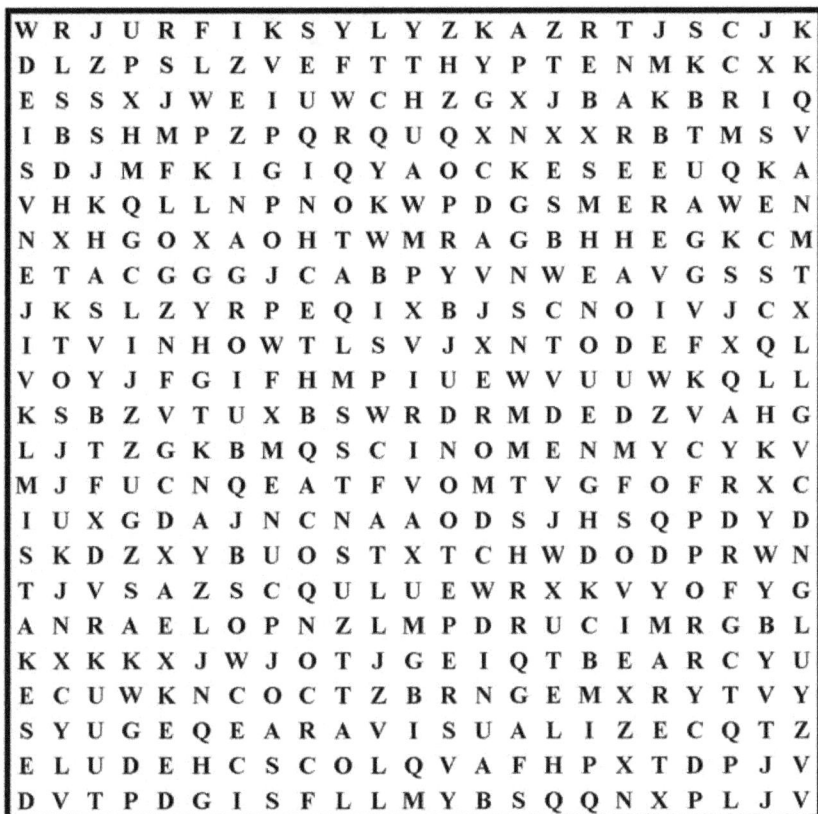

```
W R J U R F I K S Y L Y Z K A Z R T J S C J K
D L Z P S L Z V E F T T H Y P T E N M K C X K
E S S X J W E I U W C H Z G X J B A K B R I Q
I B S H M P Z P Q R Q U Q X N X X R B T M S V
S D J M F K I G I Q Y A O C K E S E E U Q K A
V H K Q L L N P N O K W P D G S M E R A W E N
N X H G O X A O H T W M R A G B H H E G K C M
E T A C G G J C A B P Y V N W E A V G S S T
J K S L Z Y R P E Q I X B J S C N O I V J C X
I T V I N H O W T L S V J X N T O D E F X Q L
V O Y J F G I F H M P I U E W V U U W K Q L L
K S B Z V T U X B S W R D R M D E D Z V A H G
L J T Z G K B M Q S C I N O M E N M Y C Y K V
M J F U C N Q E A T F V O M T V G F O F R X C
I U X G D A J N C N A A O D S J H S Q P D Y D
S K D Z X Y B U O S T X T C H W D O D P R W N
T J V S A Z S C Q U L U E W R X K V Y O F Y G
A N R A E L O P N Z L M P D R U C I M R G B L
K X K K X J W J O T J G E I Q T B E A R C Y U
E C U W K N C O C T Z B R N G E M X R Y T V Y
S Y U G E Q E A R A V I S U A L I Z E C Q T Z
E L U D E H C S C O L Q V A F H P X T D P J V
D V T P D G I S F L L M Y B S Q Q N X P L J V
```

breaks	memory	schedule
calm	mistakes	study
confidence	mnemonics	studyspot (study spot)
exams	organize	techniques
learn	review	visualize

Chapter 15
FOR SIXTH GRADERS SWITCHING CLASSES: How to Manage Your Time Between Passing Periods in Sixth Grade

Hey there, sixth-grade time manager! Switching classes, going to your locker, and squeezing in a bathroom break can feel like a race against the clock. Sixth grade often means more freedom but also more responsibility to get where you need to go—on time. The good news is that with some smart strategies, you can manage it all without feeling rushed or stressed. This chapter is packed with tips, tricks, and real-life scenarios to help you handle the hustle between classes like a pro. Let's get started!

1. Know Your Schedule Like the Back of Your Hand
Your schedule is your roadmap. Memorize the order of your classes and where each one is located. Knowing your route helps you avoid unnecessary detours.

Real-Life Scenario:
You realize your math class is on the opposite side of the school from science. Instead of wandering, you memorize the quickest path and shave two minutes off your travel time. Those two minutes are perfect for grabbing a drink from the water fountain!

2. Practice Your Locker Combo
Your locker is your base camp, but it can also be a time-eater if you're fumbling with the combination. Practice opening your locker until you can do it quickly and confidently.

Real-Life Scenario:
On the first day, you forget your locker combo and spend five minutes panicking. By the end of the week, after practicing a few times each day, you can open it in under 30 seconds. Now you've got plenty of time to swap books and head to class.

3. Plan Locker Stops Wisely

You don't need to visit your locker between every class. Plan your stops so you only go when absolutely necessary—like when you need to switch out books or grab supplies.

Real-Life Scenario:

You realize you can grab everything you need for history and science at the same time, so you skip your locker stop after history. Instead, you head straight to the restroom and still make it to science with time to spare.

4. Keep Your Locker Organized

A messy locker is a timewaster. Organize your books, binders, and supplies so you can grab what you need without digging through a pile of stuff.

Real-Life Scenario:

You keep your math and English books on one shelf and your science and history supplies on another. When it's time to grab your math textbook, you know exactly where it is and don't waste time searching.

5. Map Out Bathroom Breaks

You probably won't have time to hit the restroom between every class, so plan your breaks around when it's most convenient—like after a class that's close to the restroom.

Real-Life Scenario:

You notice the restroom is right next to your gym class, so you make it a habit to stop there after P.E. This saves you from rushing to the bathroom later when the hallways are packed.

6. Don't Linger in the Hallways

It's tempting to chat with friends or walk slowly while checking your phone, but those precious minutes add up. Focus on getting to your destination first—then talk or scroll later.

Real-Life Scenario:

You see your friend near their locker and start chatting, but realize you only have two minutes left. You say, "Catch you at lunch!" and head to class. You make it on time and avoid getting in trouble.

7. Carry the Right Supplies

Keep essential items, like a pencil case, tissues, or your agenda in your backpack so you don't have to make extra trips to your locker.

Real-Life Scenario:

You forget to grab a pencil from your locker before heading to math class. After that, you start carrying a small pencil pouch in your backpack, so you're always prepared.

8. Pay Attention to the Bell Schedule

Some schools give different amounts of time between classes, so know how much time you have and use it wisely. If you only have three minutes, every second counts.

Real-Life Scenario:

You notice that lunch ends with a three-minute bell, but morning classes have five minutes between them. You use the extra morning time to organize your locker, so you're ready for the busier afternoon.

9. Use Your Time Efficiently

Walking with purpose (not running!) helps you get to your next class quickly. Avoid stopping for unnecessary detours and stay focused.

Real-Life Scenario:
You realize the quickest route from English to gym is through the main hallway, even though it's crowded. Instead of stopping to chat with friends by the lockers, you weave through the crowd and make it to gym on time.

10. Ask for Help When You Need It

If you're confused about your schedule or can't find a classroom, don't waste time wandering—ask a teacher or a classmate for help.

Real-Life Scenario:
On the first day, you struggle to locate your art class and begin to feel anxious. You ask a teacher in the hallway, and they show you a shortcut. From then on, you know exactly where to go.

11. Avoid Overpacking Your Backpack

Carrying too much stuff slows you down and makes your transitions harder. Only pack what you need for the next class or two.

Real-Life Scenario:
You used to carry all your books all day, which made your backpack heavy and your transitions slow. Now, you only take what you need for two classes at a time and walking between rooms is much easier.

12. Stay Calm and Focused
Rushing around can make you feel stressed and forget things. Take a deep breath, focus on what you need to do, and move with purpose.

Real-Life Scenario:
You forget your science binder and start panicking. Instead of running back to your locker, you calmly tell your teacher. They let you grab it after class, and you learn to double-check next time.

13. Be Ready for the Unexpected
Sometimes, the hallways are extra crowded, or a teacher stops you to chat. Build a little buffer time into your routine so small delays don't throw you off.

Real-Life Scenario:
You leave your locker 30 seconds earlier than usual, which helps you avoid a bottleneck at the stairs. You make it to class on time, even with the extra hallway traffic.

Final Thought
Managing your time between classes in sixth grade is about being prepared, being organized, and keeping your cool. By planning ahead and focusing on your priorities, you can navigate the busiest hallways, tackle locker stops, and still make it to class with time to spare. So get ready to own those transitions like a sixth-grade time management pro. You've got this!

Chapter 15 For Sixth Graders Switching Classes...

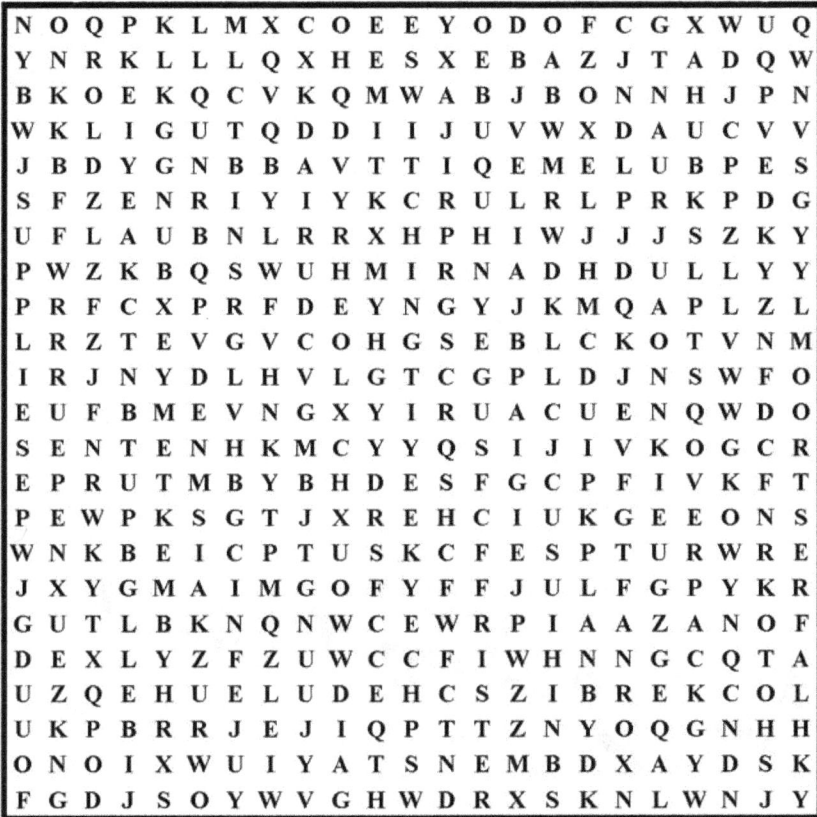

```
N O Q P K L M X C O E E Y O D O F C G X W U Q
Y N R K L L L Q X H E S X E B A Z J T A D Q W
B K O E K Q C V K Q M W A B J B O N N H J P N
W K L I G U T Q D D I I J U V W X D A U C V V
J B D Y G N B B A V T T I Q E M E L U B P E S
S F Z E N R I Y I Y K C R U L R L P R K P D G
U F L A U B N L R R X H P H I W J J J S Z K Y
P W Z K B Q S W U H M I R N A D H D U L L Y Y
P R F C X P R F D E Y N G Y J K M Q A P L Z L
L R Z T E V G V C O H G S E B L C K O T V N M
I R J N Y D L H V L G T C G P L D J N S W F O
E U F B M E V N G X Y I R U A C U E N Q W D O
S E N T E N H K M C Y Y Q S I J I V K O G C R
E P R U T M B Y B H D E S F G C P F I V K F T
P E W P K S G T J X R E H C I U K G E E O N S
W N K B E I C P T U S K C F E S P T U R W R E
J X Y G M A I M G O F Y F F J U L F G P Y K R
G U T L B K N Q N W C E W R P I A A Z A N O F
D E X L Y Z F Z U W C C F I W H N N G C Q T A
U Z Q E H U E L U D E H C S Z I B R E K C O L
U K P B R R J E J I Q P T T Z N Y O Q G N H H
O N O I X W U I Y A T S N E M B D X A Y D S K
F G D J S O Y W V G H W D R X S K N L W N J Y
```

bell
classes
efficiently
hallways
linger

locker
organized
overpack
plan
restroom

schedule
supplies
switching
time
wandering

CHAMPION#1

Word Search Solutions

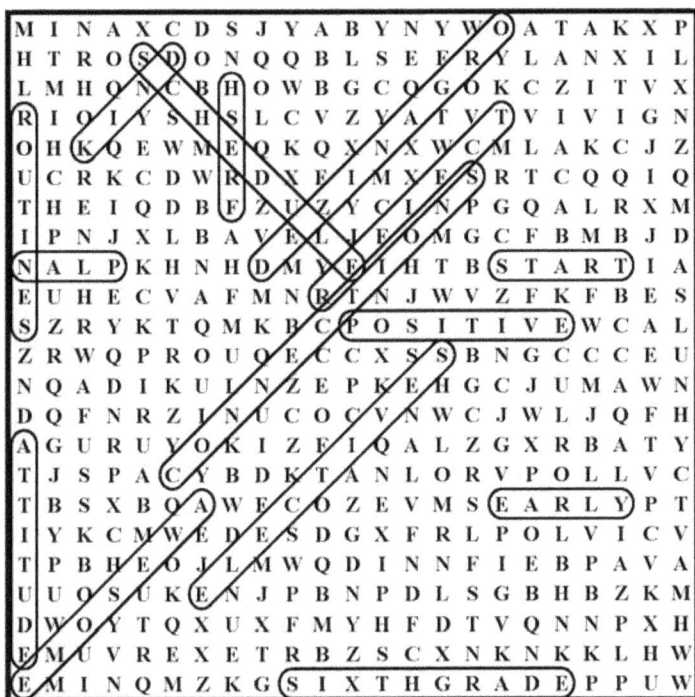

```
A K F I Q S C F Z Q B V Y A B Q D F A O S D P
R S K L W B E H O T Q T D T B M H L J T R E W
U T G D E E A N X X J P H X J P T M A H C C A
H V F B Q S A Y O P T E B X T C X N U E B N L
T Y W I S H R X J X X J V S S E D T U R J A K
P Y X U O X F U M O N K L E B U Z S G S H L A
I P F I L B A R O S L V S A P U Q Y T U Q A W
V N W H B U R O I Y B B P Y S Z N M I P B B A
U T Z Z U P B R R E L T C O N F I D E N T G Y
H F G B Z G O G C L N Y S J D V N I O T S I C
L R V T A C C L R K G D D E S Z D W S R Y Q R
S A Q S Z G H A R D H X S F E B Z P Q W L A T
X K I Z F S M Z F K P E U C G U I C W N H H Q
M D A W I K T L B A T T H L T H N S A I G N K
T H R X K F R C Z V U A P I S C T U W I T N S
E X E A E S E I E D L R O D P T E P R U C Z V
O C S G M O A M E L I B N P A K R P G O F I S
S E I Y D A T G E Y B E G W M P E O T U X M P
B Z X T X O C N P V I L E N W R S R I N P H N
G I D M S V G R I R H E K C Q P T T J I K L P
X V Y S Q E G A F I X C U Y X Z O A R D T T S
N P A W G V E I B U V I C B K H K N L X E G D
C K I L B N G K F P B U W Z U P I V W B O D M
```

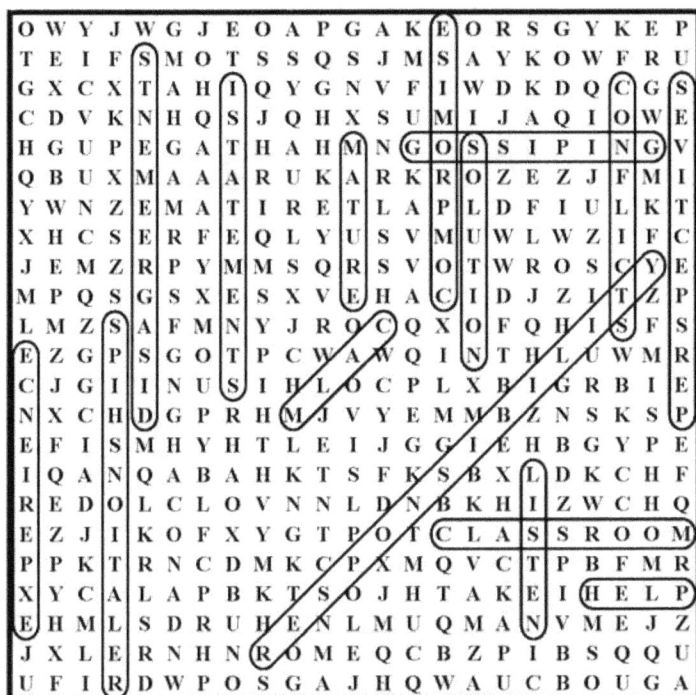

```
L Q A I U O N B X G F R V L G Q W S E H U P L
H U D B U V Q K E J K L L G M U R T P A F T E
U L S Q P U I I J W C Z Y Q O P C X W N P H Z
M V I Z F S Z N N A D W M I K A T E E G A A I
O M O T I X N T F M M Z W A M Z P R W O E N G
R V A J D R G N I S S U C S I D G V R U T D O
F F B T E N X W Y C X A M I X S S N C T I L L
M G I D I N Z F U J R J G Y Q S D C U S O E O
Z N H I V K R Z E S I U T F W G L R D V H J P
P C I Z B N V Y Y G Z L Q P F W K I K Y E E A
Q E G Z A M H A P R A F Y C H C J R E Z Z G O
Q V A N D X I U S Y C N R L M V J S T O R S V
E X R C N N L E T G O C G N W G L V V E B S N
G B G X T L N R A E D I S T U O Z N E H M F Y
P L U I J V C H W X C B X Z E L K V Q C N O S
J R M R F E Y S O V L M U O R X O C S C C J W
P D E W I D I A S E H S N G M V E J V U C R
Z L N N L A V K S T Z S H N Y U O H J V H C E
A H T S D J F N A L C C X C H I N S X M E A V
Q B M N D D W E Z J G S H Z T U W R X M S A I
K T F N F P B L A M I N G O I P P N X A A J D
N K T E A M O O N W J G M G T S V J U I I I O
E V I G R O F M O N V E Z U Z A T B H N D J K
```

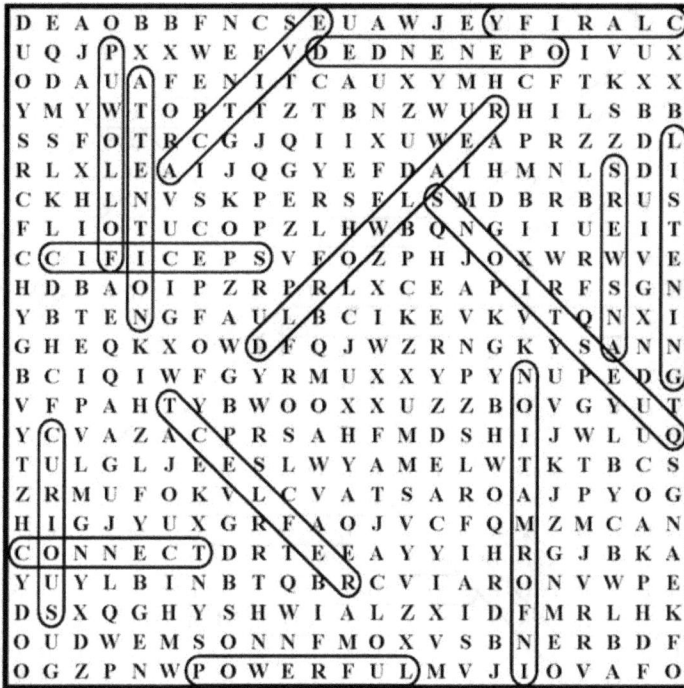

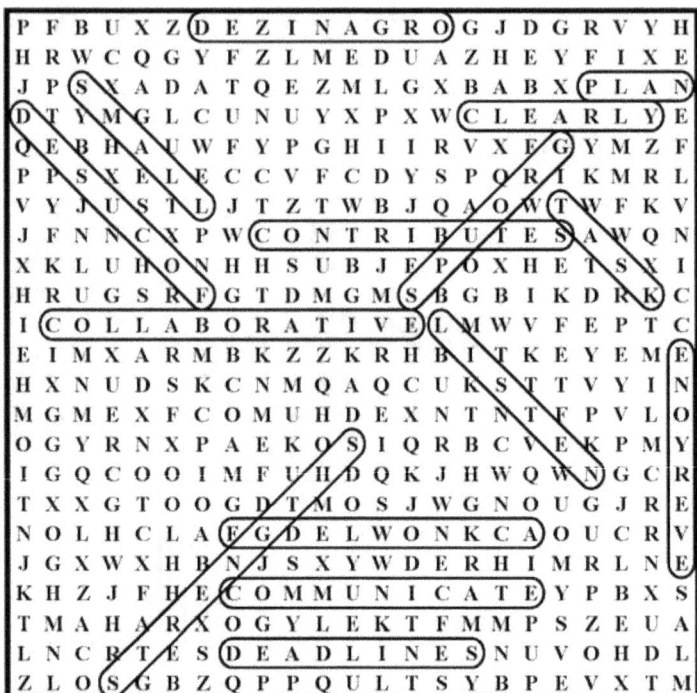

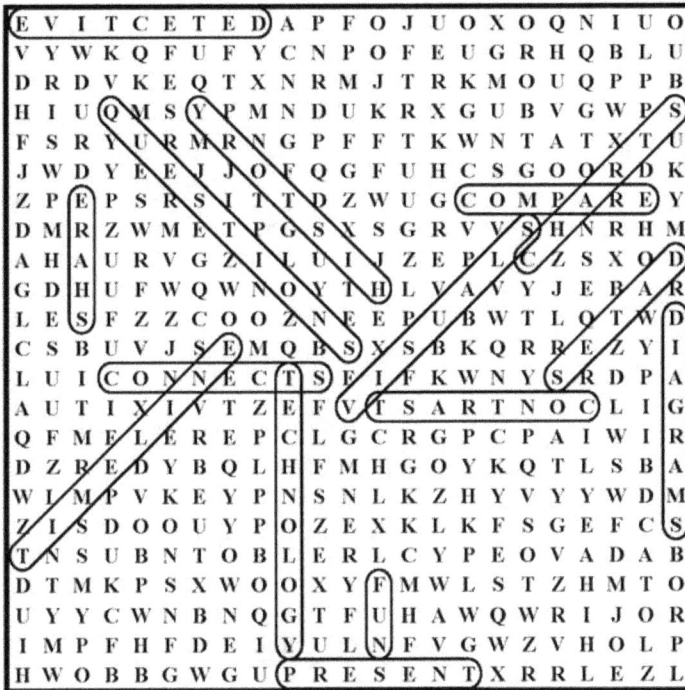

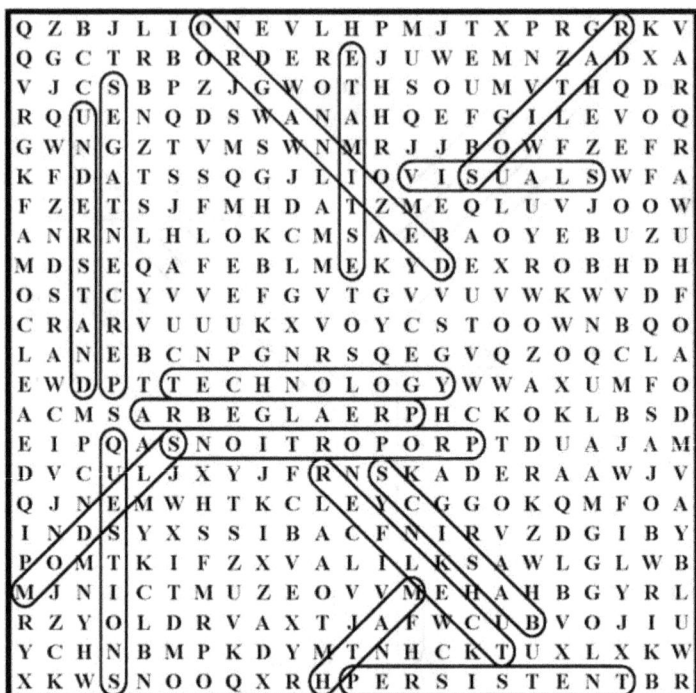

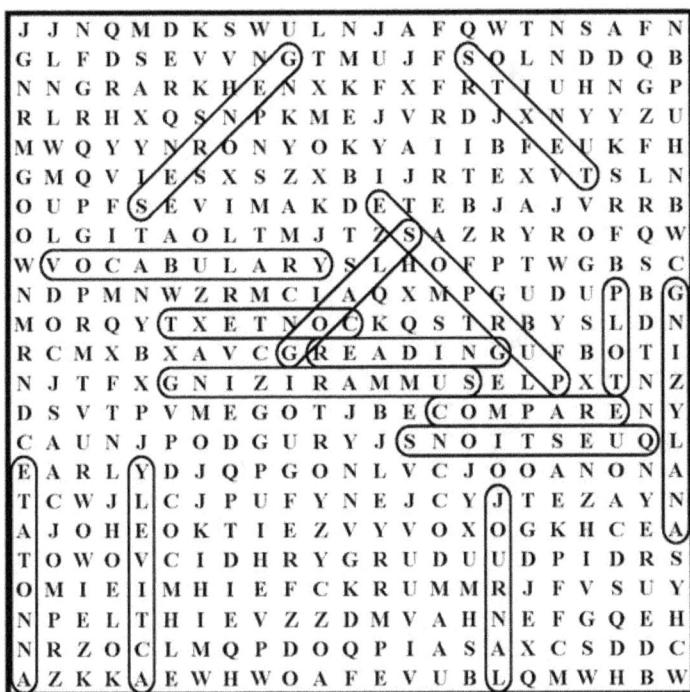

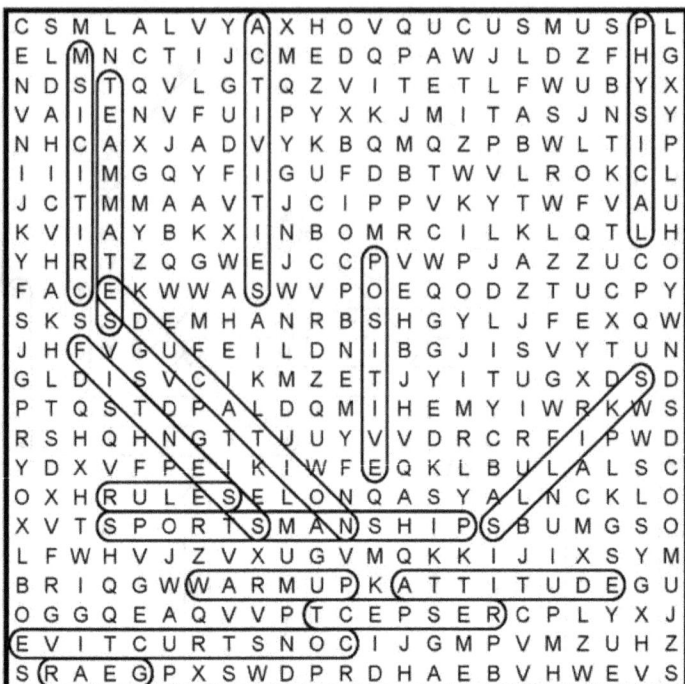

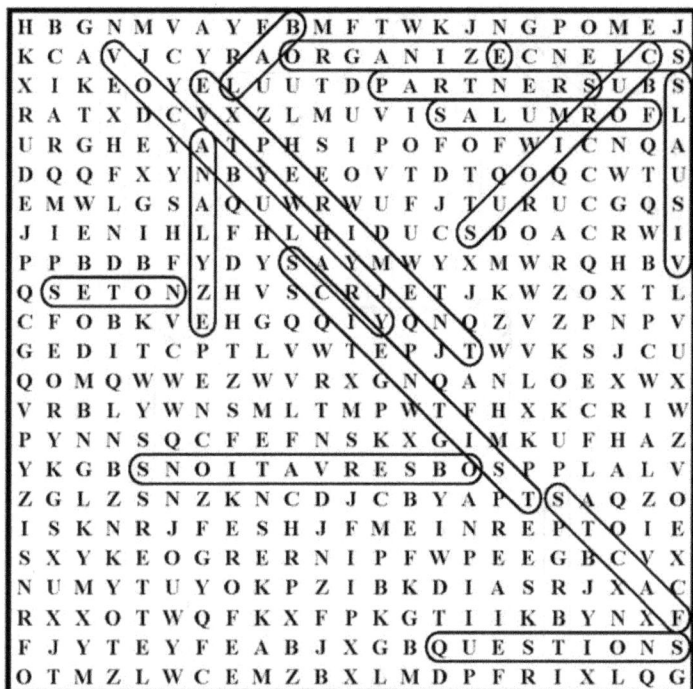

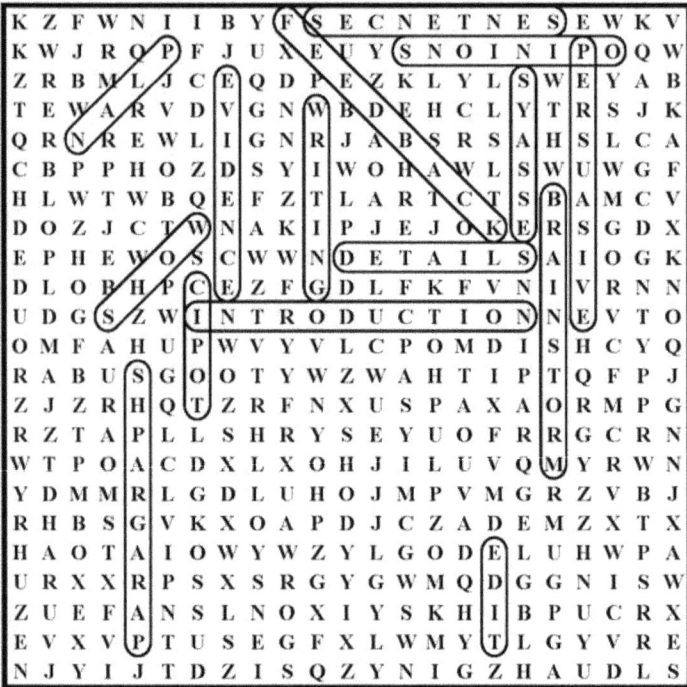

```
K  Z  F  W  N  I  I  B  Y  F  S  E  C  N  E  T  N  E  S  E  W  K  V
K  W  J  R  O  P  F  J  U  X  E  U  Y  S  N  O  I  N  I  P  O  Q  W
Z  R  B  M  L  J  C  E  Q  D  P  E  Z  K  L  Y  L  S  W  E  Y  A  B
T  E  W  A  R  V  D  V  G  N  W  B  D  E  H  C  L  Y  T  R  S  J  K
Q  R  N  E  W  L  I  G  N  R  J  A  B  S  R  S  A  H  S  L  C  A
C  B  P  P  H  O  Z  D  S  Y  I  W  O  H  A  W  L  S  W  U  W  G  F
H  L  W  T  W  B  Q  E  F  Z  T  L  A  R  T  C  T  S  B  A  M  C  V
D  O  Z  J  C  T  W  N  A  K  I  P  J  E  J  O  K  E  R  S  G  D  X
E  P  H  E  W  O  S  C  W  W  N  D  E  T  A  I  L  S  A  I  O  G  K
D  L  O  B  H  P  C  E  Z  F  G  D  L  F  K  F  V  N  I  V  R  N  N
U  D  G  S  Z  W  I  N  T  R  O  D  U  C  T  I  O  N  N  E  V  T  O
O  M  F  A  H  U  P  W  V  Y  V  L  C  P  O  M  D  I  S  H  C  Y  Q
R  A  B  U  S  G  O  O  T  Y  W  Z  W  A  H  T  I  P  T  Q  F  P  J
Z  J  Z  R  H  Q  T  Z  R  F  N  X  U  S  P  A  X  A  O  R  M  P  G
R  Z  T  A  P  L  L  S  H  R  Y  S  E  Y  U  O  F  R  R  G  C  R  N
W  T  P  O  A  C  D  X  L  X  O  H  J  I  L  U  V  Q  M  Y  R  W  N
Y  D  M  M  R  L  G  D  L  U  H  O  J  M  P  V  M  G  R  Z  V  B  J
R  H  B  S  G  V  K  X  O  A  P  D  J  C  Z  A  D  E  M  Z  X  T  X
H  A  O  T  A  I  O  W  Y  W  Z  Y  L  G  O  D  E  L  U  H  W  P  A
U  R  X  X  R  P  S  X  S  R  G  Y  G  W  M  Q  D  G  G  N  I  S  W
Z  U  E  F  A  N  S  L  N  O  X  I  Y  S  K  H  I  B  P  U  C  R  X
E  V  X  V  P  T  U  S  E  G  F  X  L  W  M  Y  T  L  G  Y  V  R  E
N  J  Y  I  J  T  D  Z  I  S  Q  Z  Y  N  I  G  Z  H  A  U  D  L  S
```

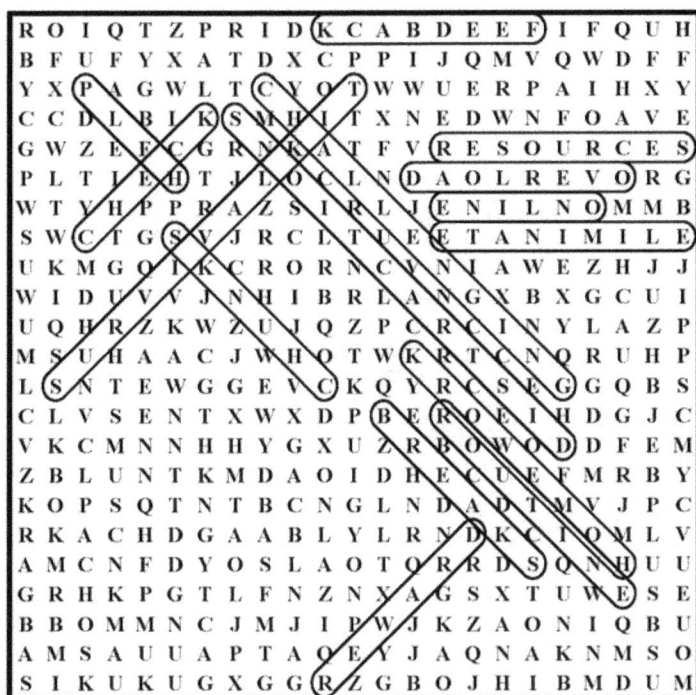

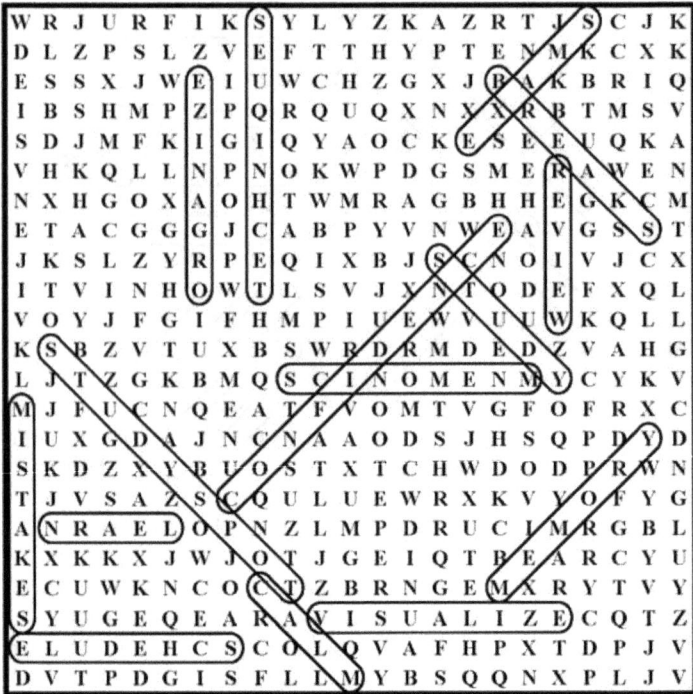

```
N O Q P K L M X C O E E Y O D O F C G X W U Q
Y N R K L L L Q X H E S X E B A Z J T A D Q W
B K O E K Q C V K Q M W A B J B O N N H J P N
W K L I G U T Q D D I I J U V W X D A U C V V
J B D Y G N B B A V T T I Q E M E L U B P E S
S F Z E N R I Y I Y K C R U L R L P R K P D G
U F L A U B N L R R X H P H I W J J J S Z K Y
P W Z K B Q S W U H M I R N A D H D U L L Y Y
P R F C X P R F D E Y N G Y J K M Q A P L Z L
L R Z T E V G V C O H G S E B L C K O T V N M
I R J N Y D L H V L G T C G P L D J N S W F O
E U F B M E V N G X Y I R U A C U E N Q W D O
S E N T E N H K M C Y Y Q S I J I V K O G C R
E P R U T M B Y B H D E S F G C P F I V K F T
P E W P K S G T J X R E H C I U K G E E O N S
W N K B E I C P T U S K C F E S P T U R W R E
J X Y G M A I M G O F Y F F J U L F G P Y K R
G U T L B K N Q N W C E W R P I A A Z A N O F
D E X L Y Z F Z U W C C F I W H N N G C Q T A
U Z Q E H U E L U D E H C S Z I B R E K C O L
U K P B R R J E J I Q P T T Z N Y O Q G N H H
O N O I X W U I Y A T S N E M B D X A Y D S K
F G D J S O Y W V G H W D R X S K N L W N J Y
```

143

Other Books by Bobbie Anderson Jr.

Third Grade Survival Guide
Fourth Grade Survival Guide
Fifth Grade Survival Guide